Prologue

~

If we could tell the story of how much God loves us, what words would we use? How would we choose to express the incredible sense of longing our creator has for us? Would we use words like eternal, unending, unfathomable? To use these mortal words to describe a love so vast is to place a limit on our God's love that could never contain it. So perhaps we cannot convey how much God loves us, but surely, we can describe the way in which he loves us. He sees us as pure and innocent...the epitome of all that is good and wonderful...we are, after all, His Beloved...His Creation. Yet even these words fall short. In truth, we have no words to describe the love of God. We have no way of knowing what God was feeling when He determined to create us, but we do know, beyond the shadow of any doubt, that He loves us. We may not be able to describe this love, or even to understand it, but we feel it. We know it's there because each and every day since the moment our Lord and savior entered our lives we have felt something that we never knew before and something that we cannot explain. Even now as I struggle for words to convey the sentiment I am trying to express, I can only stop and wonder, "How much does God love me?" It's with these limitations that I venture forth and try to put into writing anything that could describe the love that God has for us. We are more precious to Him than anything else in all of His creation. I hope my words that follow convey in some small sense, what you mean to the heavenly father. If you do not know this love I so humanly attempt to describe, I hope that by the time you finish reading this you do. It is my prayer that these words somehow steer you to a relationship with the Creator Himself, because that, above all else, is what His love does for us...it breaks our hearts for those who do not know Him.

It is in this last statement that I come to the second purpose of this journey. To experience a love so unimaginable as the love our Lord has for us is not something that we can keep to ourselves. While His love is unconditional and requires no merit to earn, we cannot experience this love without, in turn, showing that love to others. The moment that Christ begins to operate in our lives, He begins to share His heart with us. Little by little, we begin to see our world the way Christ sees it. We begin to look at others the way Christ views His bride. We do not have the capacity to love others the way that God loves us, but we do have the capacity to love them, and to introduce them to the unexplainable love of our Savior. As the apostle John wrote, "We love because He first loved us."[1]

~

Part One

The Beginning

~

She was perfect. Nothing else in creation existed like her. The heavenly beings created eternities before stared in amazement at her. She was pure and innocent, perfect in every way, and He loved her more than any of His other creations. He placed her in perfection and lavished her with everything she could ever desire. No need went unmet. He walked with her in the garden that He provided for her and spent the days talking with her. She loved Him with a love that only innocence could produce, and one that only His love for her could overshadow. He cherished her. She was His beloved.

~

Chapter 1
In His Image

~

The only sensible place to begin exploring the love of
the Creator is at creation...or is it? As we take this trip
back to the beginning, it's important for us to
acknowledge the beginning of our existence was not
the beginning of God. This is the first mental hurdle
that we encounter as we try to wrap our mortal minds
around the love of God. God's love eclipses all time
and space because God Himself eclipses all time and
space. If we were to claim that God's love was
"unfathomable", which means incapable of being fully
explored or understood, then the God whose love is
unfathomable must also be unfathomable. This concept
is hard to grasp for created beings because all we know
is creation. Everything in our lives, save God, exists
within the confines of His creation. Our understanding
of time, of our earth, of our solar systems, of our
bodies, and everything else exists only within the
understanding of the created. As we push further and
further into space and discover new and amazing
things, we find fewer and fewer answers, while at the
same time uncovering more and more questions.
When we do answer one single question, that answer
unlocks the door to a thousand new questions. This is
exactly how God's love is.

When we first encounter God, we can't explain what
we feel. We begin to feel a tug at our hearts, a nervous

feeling in our chest. We realize that something is happening, but we don't know what. All of a sudden, the moment that Christ enters our lives, a sense of belonging that we can't comprehend, yet alone explain, overcomes us. The current of God's love is so strong and great that it sweeps us up and all we can do is enjoy the ride. It's at this moment, when we first recognize the love of the father, that everything begins to change. It's now when we begin questioning. We wonder how God can love us sinners. We don't deserve this great and wonderful love. Nothing about God's love is deserved, but one of the greatest qualities of God is that He does not care what we deserve, He loves us!

The book of Genesis tends to be where our minds can begin to attempt to understand our existence, and in turn, God's love for us. Prior to Genesis 1:1, "In the beginning, God created…"[2] we have absolutely zero concept of what was going on. God was there, the uncreated, in nothingness. Just God…all God. Even as I write this, I can't get my mind to grasp it. Countless unknowns exist that our created brains cannot even begin to process about the uncreated, and since we can't even determine what was happening at that point, we need to focus on what we know. So, let's start "in the beginning."

When God decided to create our world, He created it with an order that only a divine creator could establish. He did everything in just the right order, so that all of the miracles of His creation would exist in perfect harmony together. Day one, heavens and earth, light and dark. Day two, sky. Day three, land and plants. Day four, the sun, moon, and stars. Day five, fish and birds. Day six, animals and man. Day six...

The very first mention of God's love is not a word that translates into love in any way. There is no deep hidden meaning of the Hebrew words that are used to describe day six that suggest any type of love. However, when we read Genesis 1:26, we see God's love in the difference of how man was created. "Let us make mankind in our likeness, in our image..."[3]. Think about this statement and your life today. We are all very different people, but if you really consider your friends and the people that you are close to, what do you see? Commonality. You surround yourself with people that you have things in common with, because you want relationships. If you have absolutely nothing in common with a person, you can be civil and polite and potentially even enjoy time together on a temporary basis, but you can never have a relationship. God wants us to be in a relationship with Him, and what better way to develop a relationship with your creation than to make them like you.

We glean a second glimpse of God's love from this phrase that seems slightly less relational but isn't. You and I are created in the likeness of the Almighty God. WOW. Nothing else, in all of God's expansive creation can claim that it was created in the image of God, except for us. God didn't create anything else like Him. Not angels, not animals, not fish, not birds, not particles, not celestial bodies. He created us in His image. Why would he do that? Why would he create us in His image? The second part of Genesis 1:26 tells us…"so that they may rule…"[3] God created us in His image so that we could rule over all of His other creations. We have been given authority and dominion over all of creation because God has authority and dominion over all of creation. We are His children, and He has given us everything because He loves us! This basic understanding, and I do stress the word basic, of creation offers us a peek into the incredible love that our God has for us. As we move forward, everything else will be based on this one moment, this one instance, where God created us in His image.

~

Chapter 2
Perfection

~

It's difficult to really comprehend the wonder of Eden. Imagine the beauty and perfection of a garden planted by God. My mind always goes to the images of James Hilton's Shangri La[4] or Homer's Elysian Fields[5]. These fictional images of an earthly type of paradise cannot rival Eden though. Eden was real and created by God. Similar to God's love, His creation is impossible to truly understand or replicate. Created minds describe a utopian garden one way, but this is little more than a poor choice of words compared to the Lord's creation. Even as you read this and your mind constructs the images of lush vegetation, delectable fruit growing on flourishing trees, clean and clear rivers winding gently through the harmonious nature that existed between everything...the imagery falls so incredibly short. Our minds only devise what we know. Even the written words of the great authors of the past, whose romantic illusions so eloquently described their hidden paradise, were based completely on what they could see. God's creation is the basis for everything that we can construct, because we exist within that creation. Eden exemplified paradise for sure, but one magnificent detail made it more than a garden...it was God's garden. Throughout the first chapter of Genesis, we see God "create" and "make", but in Genesis chapter 2, God "plants" a garden. This made Eden personal. God's garden...and man was able to live in it.

Once God had planted this garden, He placed his beloved creation, the one thing He created in His image, inside the garden. This action of placing mankind in the garden, perfect creation inside of perfect creation, again shows us God's desire to be close to us. We see yet another glimpse of this in Genesis 2 when God does something, He had not yet done...He speaks to man. God had not spoken to any of His other creations. He spoke them into existence, but He had not spoken to them directly. Hearing God's spoken word was an honor reserved for man. To truly attempt understanding the relationship that God desires to have with us requires that we acknowledge the significance of this moment. God could have chosen anything, but He chose us. He created us in His image, placed us in His garden, and He spoke to us. The relationship between mankind and God had begun.

The unique nature of the relationship that God established with us was intentional. God had not been in a relationship with anything else that had ever existed until He created man. God cherished this relationship and provided immensely for man. He gave him everything he needed, and then God determined that man needed a helper. God created woman, and man was overjoyed. God did not give man the gift of companionship for no reason. The next command began the greatest love story that has ever been, or ever will be told, for it was the first concept we ever have of the Bride of Christ. God told the man and woman to be fruitful and increase in number. He wanted the earth to be filled with His creation. He wanted to have a relationship with all of mankind and for them to have a relationship with Him. He wanted to see His beloved creation flourish and grow. He wanted to spend time with them. He wanted them to love Him. He wanted His relationships to be perfect. You don't need a master's degree in Divinity Studies to know what happened after man was placed in the garden. I dare say, that no matter your level of relationship with Christ, you know the story of Eden. You are fully aware of the command by God to not eat from the Tree of Knowledge of Good and Evil and the temptations of the serpent. You know that God's wonderful creation fell. What a dark day for mankind. The Bible says in Genesis that as soon as they ate the fruit their eyes were opened and they were ashamed of their nakedness.[6.] Prior to consuming this forbidden fruit, they knew no shame. They knew only perfection because that is all they had encountered. God's creation was perfect and knew no flaw, but in order for God to have the relationship He desired, He gave mankind free will. It's this gift of free will that allows us to have a relationship with God that no other creation can have. Free will means that we can love God because we choose to love God, not because we were told to. Since the dawn of time God's creation has worshipped Him because they were created to do so. God created us to do the same, but we also have the choice to not worship. We could choose to love our wonderful God or to turn away from Him and turn away is exactly what we did. The magnificence of God's amazing love for you and I shines through in that moment. He knew this was going to happen. He knew prior to ever making the first move towards the very first creation of anything He ever created that His most prized possession would turn away. He knew that thing that He looked at and saw purity and wonder and passion was going to fade. He knew that the thing that made the most beautiful worship, because it was the most genuine worship, would walk away from Him. He knew that His Beloved would break His heart time and time again, yet He still loved us. That is perfect love, and we will never, ever be able to comprehend it.

~

Chapter 3
Heartbreak

~

The consequences of mankind's first sin reached much further than Adam and Eve. The events that followed immediately after that have always been so brutally clear about what really happened. Yes, sin entered into the world and mankind would suffer under the yoke of sin for thousands of years to follow, but what exactly took place? What was sin and what was the recourse? Sin is disobedience, but the consequence of sin is separation from God. In Genesis 3, after Adam and Eve have committed their sin, the Bible says that their eyes were opened, and they were ashamed. What is shame? Shame is a pain and humiliation resulting from doing something wrong. Shame is what God never wants His Beloved to feel. Shame is what causes us to withdraw. When we feel shame, we feel embarrassed. When we're embarrassed, we remove ourselves from a relationship. When we remove ourselves from a relationship, we hurt both parties. Adam and Eve's shame caused them to hide from God.

Imagine being in the Garden of Eden at this moment, as dreadful as it may have been, imagine, not what Adam and Eve were feeling, but what God was feeling. God walked in the garden, looking for Adam and Eve. Now, the Bible does not specifically illustrate how often this happened, or if it indeed had ever happened prior, but I personally believe it took place quite often. We have already discussed how God spoke to Adam and gave him commands, so God was obviously talking to him, but think about the nature of God and what He's done so far. He created man in His own image, personally planted a garden and placed Him in it, spoke to Him directly, recognized that He needed some help and created woman. This is not the action of someone who doesn't want to be around. This behavior typifies an intimately involved father. A creator who wants a relationship. When you desire a relationship you engage the other person. If I desire to have a relationship with my children, but I don't try to talk to them, ask them about their interests, and spend time with them, what type of relationship is that? God was no different, and that's why I love to believe that He spent hours upon hours in the garden with Adam and Eve loving and adoring His beloved children. How did He spend that time and in what form was He in? Did He come and go? I'm afraid we'll never know those details, but I believe it is safe to assume that the desire for a relationship meant that God was there.

So, back to the question. Adam and Eve hide as God is walking through the garden. How does God feel? It is so important for us to always remember that God never doesn't know what's going on. God has never experienced surprise or revelation. He's never been caught off guard. He knew exactly where Adam and Eve were and why, but He calls out to them anyway. Why? Why not just say "Hey, get out here and quit hiding!" I think of my own children so often in this story. Unfortunately, my children are familiar with right and wrong because they were born into a sinful world. I wish they didn't. I wish that their purity and innocence was perpetual. As they grow, they know what is right and they know when they've done wrong. Adam and Eve knew they had done wrong, and worse than that, they knew that God was not going to like it. They felt remorse and shame. What did God feel? Heartbreak. God's wonderful children had sinned, and God wasn't angry at the sin. His heart broke because His most cherished and prized creation doubted His unconditional love and hid. Yes, consequences had to follow, but not in anger. God's love trumped everything else, even in the face of disobedience.

If we pay close attention to what happens next, we see an amazing example of God's love. Genesis 3 tells us that after everything had happened, after the consequences had been levied[7], that God banished Adam and Eve from Eden and placed an angel with a flaming sword to guard the entrance.[8] This sounds like another consequence on the surface, but I assure you it was the greatest act of love that God could have given them. To understand why, we have to look at a few different scriptures. We'll start in verse 3 of Genesis 3. Pay attention to the serpent's words:

"You will not certainly die, for God knows that when you eat from it your eyes will be opened, and you will be like God, knowing good and evil."

Satan knew exactly what He was doing. He was playing on Eve's desires to help. Eve had been created to help Adam, to be his partner. What better way to help than to know what God knew? Eve, simply trying to help, had no malicious plan to do something horrible, but the problem still remained. Even though her intentions may have been noble, sin still existed, and the wages of sin are death. This sin brings us to Romans. Romans 5:12 says:

Therefore, just as sin entered the world through one man, and death through sin, and in this way death came to all people, because all sinned.

Stay with me. Let's jump over to 1st Corinthians. 1 Corinthians 15:24-26 says:

Then the end will come, when he hands over the kingdom to God the Father after he has destroyed all dominion, authority and power. For he must reign until he has put all his enemies under his feet. The last enemy to be destroyed is death

Last one, I promise. Back to Genesis 3. Genesis 3:22 says:

And the Lord God said, "The man has now become like one of us, knowing good and evil. He must not be allowed to reach out his hand and take also from the tree of life and eat, and live forever."

Now, let's tie this all together. When Adam and Eve sinned, death entered into this world. Every man and woman have sinned, and therefore must taste death (Unless God intervenes in a different manner like in the cases of Enoch[9] and Elijah[10], but those are different conversations for a different time). Had Adam and Eve eaten from the Tree of Life, they, nor mankind, would ever have known death. But isn't that a good thing? On the surface, it sounds great. No lost loved ones, no tragic accidents, no mourning...but just like Adam and Eve's banishment, death appears to be a punishment, when it's actually a blessing. Without death, there could be no resurrection. Had Christ not died on Calvary, He would have never walked out of the grave three days later in triumph. Death may not have reigned in the physical form, but spiritual death would have ruled for eternity. Had Adam and Eve eaten from the Tree of Life, Christ could not have died for any of us, and we would have lived an eternal life of separation from God. Adam and Eve's banishment began the rescue plan.

~

Part 2

The Rescue Plan

~

He watched as His Beloved walked away from Eden, clothed in animal skins and stained with sin, His wonderful Beloved had chosen separation from her creator. The pain, as He watched her walk further and further away, only grew as time passed. He watched evil grow inside of her more and more with each passing day. He longed for her to return. He would welcome her back in an instant...but His Beloved had turned from Him, ignored Him, blasphemed Him, and forgotten Him. The evil that had overtaken her was too great. He had to take action if there was any chance of saving her. He searched everywhere, for any sign that there may still be good in her, for any indication that she still loved Him. And then, there, in all of sin's darkness, a faint light shown through the black. The light that He had placed in her at creation had not yet been extinguished.

~

Chapter 4
The Seed

~

When sin entered into the world darkness reigned over mankind. In the roughly 1000 years since Adam was created, God had watched mankind turn into something that broke His heart. Satan had released his hordes on the earth with a single goal, to defile mankind to a point that was beyond redemption. Satan remembered all too well what God had told him in Eden after mankind's fall. Genesis 3:15 says

And I will put enmity between you and the woman, and between your offspring and hers; he will crush your head, and you will strike his heel.

Satan is evil, cunning, and a brilliant strategist. He knew that God was telling him that his end was coming. He knew that he would be destroyed by an offspring from Eve, so he set out to destroy any chance of a righteous child ever being born to mankind. He knew God had a seed, but he didn't know who the seed was or when that seed would show up. The only thing Satan could do was target everyone.

At this time, the world had become so evil that God decided to destroy everyone and everything. Genesis 6:6 says:

The Lord regretted that he had made human beings on the earth, and his heart was deeply troubled.

Evil had overtaken God's creation and He decided to wipe them from the face of the earth. Satan's plan was working so perfectly. I can almost see him, surveying his earthly kingdom smiling, with a hint of surprise, as he saw how far mankind had fallen. I wonder sometimes if even Satan felt a little bit amazed at how well he was doing. Unlike God, Satan has lost, he's not perfect, he's not all-knowing...so he can be surprised. Part of me really wonders if he anxiously watched as mankind defiled themselves over and over, wondering if it was really going to work. Perhaps he was taunting God. "Your beloved children have turned to me!" "What will you do, God? Destroy them now or allow them to continue walking with me on this earth, defiling each and every generation that follows!" But God had a plan that Satan wasn't ready for...and it started with Noah.

Reading through genealogy in the Bible can be a bit mundane. Genesis 5 chronicles the genealogy of Noah. Noah was Adam's great, great, great, great, great, great, great grandson and was born only about 75 to 80 years after Adam had died. This is one of the most fascinating things in the Bible to me because I love to think about the possibility that, Adam, the very first man that God created...the man who lived in the garden of Eden...the man who ultimately sinned and unleashed evil and death on the world, potentially recounted the story to Noah's father. Imagine Lamech, Noah's father, sitting when he was younger listening to Adam tell stories of Eden. Stories about walking with God, waking up and seeing Eve, and of how much God loved him! Only a single generation separated Noah from these stories. Now, the Bible doesn't tell us how many brothers and sisters Noah had, but it does say that Lemech had other sons and daughters. Noah had other family members who were potentially hearing these stories, but he listened and learned about our loving God.

Genesis chapter 6 says that Noah found favor in the eyes of the Lord.[11] God surveyed all of earth and found only Noah. Noah had brothers and sisters, cousins, aunts and uncles, grandparents, and who knows how many other family members that had been around to potentially hear Adam's stories, but somehow, only Noah remained faithful. Noah's familiar story has an underlying reason that explains his importance to God's plan. The time to reveal the seed who would crush Satan's head had not yet arrived. In order for God to keep His word mankind could not be destroyed. Noah may not have been the vessel by which God would save mankind, but God used him to bring forth future generations that would eventually produce the victor that God had promised and save mankind for eternity. Noah's faith in God, not only saved his family, but it ushered in a fresh start for humanity that would eventually produce a savior.

~

Chapter 5
Establishing the Order

~

What was going through Noah's mind when he stepped off the ark? A flood had just wiped away every other person on the planet with the exception of his immediate family that was on the ark with him. When he walked off of that boat, I'm sure he wondered about the next steps. The very first thing he did when he walked off of the ark though, in my mind, exemplifies why God chose him to be on the ark in the first place. He built an altar. Genesis 8:21 says:

The Lord smelled the pleasing aroma and said in his heart: "Never again will I curse the ground because of humans, even though every inclination of the human heart is evil from childhood. And never again will I destroy all living creatures, as I have done"

Noah remembered what God had done and offered thanks. He offered a sacrifice to Him and that pleased God. The sacrifice made God look at his wonderful creation once more with a full heart. He was pleased. His beloved had returned. After this act of thankfulness from Noah, God established the first of His covenants with us. While God had laid out the covenant prior to Noah entering the ark, He didn't confirm it until afterwards. God makes a promise that he will never again destroy all life by the waters of a flood[12].

God's plan didn't end at Noah though. His beloved still needed a way to return to Him. While Noah acted as the conduit to get mankind to the next phase, God had another person in line to take the next steps.

~

Anyone watching God lay out His plan for mankind probably wouldn't have seen Abraham playing much of a role. When Abraham was still Abram, he lived in a place called Ur. Ur boasted a pretty robust economy and archaeological evidence suggests that Ur potentially existed as a major city in the region at this time. Abram lived with his father, Terah, and in the book of Joshua, Joshua mentions that they worshipped many gods[13]. Abram's family lived as pagans in a pagan city. The bible doesn't specifically tell us whether or not Abram had any relationship with God prior to being called, but either way, God didn't pick Abram because he was faithful. He chose him because He knew he would be faithful in the future.

When God called Abram, he made a promise to him, just like he did with Noah prior to the flood. God told Abram in Genesis 12:1-3:

...Go from your country, your people and your father's household to the land I will show you. I will make you into a great nation, and I will bless you; I will make your name great, and you will be a blessing. I will bless those who bless you, and whoever curses you I will curse; and all peoples on earth will be blessed through you.

What a promise! God told Abram that He would do a few things in this promise. First, He would give him land. Second, He would make him a "great nation" and bless him. Third, all the people of the world would be blessed through him. God told Abram that he was going to have lots of land, lots of kids, that everyone was going to know his name, and that the world would be a better place because of him. But here is what is so amazing about Abram. He gets this amazing, very specific promise that outlined exactly what God was going to do for him, all except the destination. In God's first test of Abram's faith, He told him that He would do all of these great things but didn't tell him exactly where to go. God simply told Abram to "go to the land I will show you". Abram had no idea where. He had to trust God's guidance. Faith in God's promises can oftentimes require blindly walking and trusting God to guide you.

The second part of this promise that God uses to reveal His magnificence is the part about making Abram a great nation. Abram was called by God when he was already 75 years old. Yes, the people were living a lot longer at that time but remember that lifespans had been getting shorter and shorter each generation. One of the reasons that the genealogical records from Shem to Abram in Genesis 11 exists is to show that age was becoming more and more of a factor. While Abram did live to be 175 years old, 75 was not exactly young at that time. Not only was the journey difficult for Abram and Sarai, but they also had no children. Sarai could not have a child and had given up on being a mother.

When Abram received the promise from God that he would be the father of many nations, he simply accepted this and moved on. He accepted it so well, that he never mentioned it again for years.

~

Abram lives a pretty full life with a lot of milestones in it, but there is one event that I've always thought of as a turning point in Abram's life. An event that changed His mindset from being just a guy with a promise from God, to being a guy with a God who made him a promise. There is a seriously distinct difference in these two statements, and Abram proved he knew the difference when he met the kings of Salem and Sodom.

Abram had been quietly growing more and more powerful with each passing day. After Abram had lived in Canaan for several years a war broke out in the Valley of Siddim and Lot, Abram's nephew, was taken captive. The Bible says that Abram gathered his 318 fighting men and called on his neighbors to come and help. Abram had become such a powerful man that he mobilized an army strong enough to attack the armies that had captured Lot and defeated them. On his way back, he's met by the King of Sodom, and Melchizedek, the King of Salem. Melchizedek is an interesting character in the Bible and is only mentioned a few times, and not in great detail. The name Melchizedek means "king of righteousness", and his title King of Salem means "king of peace". Melchizedek is also said to be a "Priest of God Most High " and refers to God as El Elyon[14], God Most High. The names "King of Righteousness" and "King of

Peace" suggest that Melchizedek is someone important, but the title "Priest of God Most High" is really telling. At this time, the nation of Israel did not yet exist, and so the Levitical priesthood had not been established yet. There were not priests in the order of Aaron, no priests for the Jewish people, only a priest of God, for all people. This is foreshadowing of Christ, as we learn later on in Hebrews[15]. Melchizedek took bread and wine and spoke a blessing over Abram, after which, Abram offered him a tenth of everything he had won in battle.

After this, the King of Sodom approached Abram. The King of Sodom told Abram that he could keep all of the spoils he recovered, as long as the people were returned to the King of Sodom. Abram's responds in Genesis 14:22-23:

With raised hands I have sworn an oath to the Lord, God Most High, Creator of heaven and earth, that I will accept nothing belonging to you, not even a thread or the strap of a sandal, so that you will never be able to say, 'I made Abram rich.'

Abram knew that it was God who made him a promise and that honoring God was far more important than earning rewards. God had promised to enrich Abram. Abram could have potentially been justified in thinking this was God's provision, but risking man taking credit for what God had done was not an option. Abram wanted God to be glorified above everything else, even above his own fame and riches.

~

After returning from this encounter, Abram finally asks God about His promises that he had been given. Abram faithfully trusted God and demonstrated this trust wonderfully, but a lingering question existed in Abram's mind. In Genesis 15:2, Abram says to God:

Sovereign Lord, what can you give me since I remain childless and the one who will inherit my estate is Eliezer of Damascus?" And Abram said, "You have given me no children; so a servant in my household will be my heir."

This is the first time that Abram asks God about this part of the promise. Having children was not only a part of the promise God had given Abram, but it was also something that Abram and Sarai both intimately desired. They had no children to love, to teach, to watch grow. They had family and servants, but no children of their own. God responds to Abram with the second covenant between God and man. God tells Abram that his heir would spring from his own flesh and blood, not his servant's, and then tells Abram to bring him a cow, a goat, and a ram[16].

At this time in history, written contracts between people who entered into an agreement did not exist. When making a deal, the two parties split an animal down the middle and walk between the two halves. This sealed the covenant between the two parties. God asked Abram to lay out these animals as a sign that they were about to enter into a covenant. Abram, not ignorant of this process, understood the gravity of his actions. God wanted to enter into a binding contract with Abram, and Abram took this seriously. Genesis says that after Abram had arranged the animals, birds of prey came and tried to eat them, but Abram continually chased them off[17]. Abram did not let anything defile this arrangement. That night, a dark and terrifying cloud came over Abram and he saw a "blazing fire pot and a smoking torch" pass between the two halves of the animals[18]. God had sealed the contract. Abram didn't have to walk through because God handled the entire deal. God's covenant with Abram was a unilateral contract, which meant that there was nothing that Abram had to do but trust in God. Abram had faith that God would fulfill His promises to him because he knew that God was bigger than the promise.

~

Abram possessed a great faith, but even men of great faith can slip up on occasion. After God entered into Covenant with Abram, Abram grew impatient. He had been promised an heir but had been waiting for 15 years on this promise. He knew God was capable of handling this situation but decided to try and speed things up. Abram and Sarai decided that Abram should have a child with Sarai's servant, Hagar, and so he did[19]. Hagar conceived Ismael and Abram loved him. Abram was finally happy with his child, but God said this is not the one He chose to carry forth the plan. God made a promise to Abram and He didn't need Abram's help to fulfill the promise.

A few years later, God appeared to Abram and told him again that He will make a great nation out of him[20]. God changed Abram's to Abraham and Sarai's to Sara, and Sara finally became pregnant. Imagine how excited she was. She had watched her servant produce a son that Abraham loved, yet she had not been able to provide Abraham with a child herself. Now everything was changing. She gave birth to a son that she loved more than life, a son that Abraham loved more than anything else, and a son that God had miraculously blessed them with to fulfill the promises that He had made to Abraham. Sara and Abraham named the child Isaac, and it was Isaac that God used to carry forward His plan[21].

~

Several years after Isaac was born, God told Abraham to do something that any parent would consider unthinkable. God told Abraham to offer Isaac as a burnt offering to Him[22]. Imagine Abraham's reaction. He remained patient and faithful for years. He demonstrated repeatedly how much he trusted God, and yet he was still asked to have more and more faith. I can picture Abraham crying out to God "Why?! Have I not done enough for you? Have I not proven myself to you?" I can't even begin to imagine the fear, apprehension and uncertainty that Abraham must have felt. And what about Sara??!! Can you imagine when Abraham told Sara that he would take her only son to sacrifice him? I dare say that her reaction did not convey acceptance. While Abraham and Sara shared in the heartbreak and fear of this request, they remained faithful, and Abraham followed through with what

God commanded.

While we often remember the story of Abraham and Isaac on Mount Moriah as a testament to Abraham's faith, and rightly so, we often forget about the faith of Isaac himself. In most illustrations of this story, we see Isaac as a small child, but this is most likely not an accurate visualization. The Bible doesn't specifically state Isaac's age so there is really no way to know, but there are a few contextual clues in Genesis that suggest that Isaac was aware of the situation unfolding. Abraham, Isaac, and two servants traveled for 3 days to Mount Moriah[23], suggesting Isaac was old enough to make a long journey. Next, Isaac carried the firewood up the mountain[24], enough firewood to consume the entire sacrifice, so we assume he was strong enough to do this. Finally, he recognized all of the materials and perceived enough to ask about the animal[25], so he understood the process of making a sacrifice to the Lord. Now, none of these things prove that Isaac was grown, but they do suggest that he wasn't a toddler. When Abraham bound Isaac and lay him on the altar, Isaac most likely knew what was about to happen.

Now whether Isaac kicked and screamed or not, we don't know, but we do know that he ended up on an altar with his father standing over him, willing to sacrifice his own son. The bible says that the angel of the Lord stopped Abraham and then Abraham saw a ram caught in the thicket and used it as a sacrifice[26]. Try to picture in your mind the reaction of both Abraham and Isaac when they saw that ram. I know Abraham was ecstatic, but I have to believe that Isaac was probably a little more pumped when the ram showed up. This entire event solidified Abraham's faith, and God acknowledged that Abraham loved Him more than anything else and was pleased. The other thing it did was set in Isaac's mind that God had a plan. Abraham knew one crucial piece of information that Isaac didn't during this whole time...God's promise that Isaac would produce the nations that Abraham had been promised[27]. While this knowledge didn't make the situation any easier for Abraham, he at least held onto God's promise. He could, if nothing else, say "God, you told me I would be the father of many nations through Isaac. You promised that was going to happen, so even if I go through with this sacrifice, Isaac has to be around to produce offspring. I'm not sure how you will accomplish this, but you said you would." Isaac didn't have that same level of comfort. He was under the knife, literally, and all he knew at the time was that his father loved him and trusted God. But once the ram showed up, Isaac knew that God was Jehovah Jireh...he was God the provider and he would provide for Isaac just like he provided for Abraham.

Much like the contract God made with Noah, God's covenant with Abraham required absolutely nothing special on behalf of man, it required only faith. God's great and wonderful love for us requires no work on our part. The only thing that God ever asks of us is for us to love and believe in Him. If He tells us that He will do something, He will. Abraham and Noah both received promises from God that they saw fulfilled in their lifetimes. Each man also received promises fulfilled in future generations. God's plan to redeem mankind required these two men to believe that they were being used for something greater than they would ever witness. When I was in high school, my youth pastor told me that we were "playing with eternity". That comment has always stuck with me. Everything that we do in our life has eternal consequences. Every conversation we have and every action we take echoes through eternity because we are charged with sharing God's love with every single person. We are the ones representing this perfect and wonderful love to the others in our lives. We've been given an incredible love from an incredible God and that love comes with no strings attached, but this love is so great, we have a responsibility to tell everyone about it.

~

Chapter 6
Foundations

~

Jacob's name literally means "heel grabber" and from the moment he was born he exemplified that name. The Bible says that he was actually born grasping his twin brother Esau's heel. I have always been somewhat perplexed at the whole concept of "heel grabbing". I mean, I get it, if you grab someone's heel, you're trying to slow them down or impede their progress, but honestly, why the heel? If I'm chasing you and want to slow you down, I'm probably not going for the heel. Anyway, musing over. Almost half of Jacob's life can be summed up with this one name. From birth, Jacob was looking out for himself and he wasn't worried about who he had to double cross. The Bible said that while his brother Esau was an outdoors man who hunted and worked in the fields, Jacob was quiet and stayed in the tents. Shrewd and cunning, Jacob always seemed to be working some sort of angle. When Esau came home hungry from a hunting trip, Jacob actually talked Esau into trading his spiritual birthright to him in exchange for a bowl of soup[28]. The whole decision on Esau's part to enter into such a transaction aside, Jacob was tricky and a bit dishonest.

Jacob inherited dishonesty from his mother, Rebekah, who was a bit of a go getter herself. She possessed initiative and drive and showed it from the moment Abraham's servant encountered her at the well in

Nahor[29]. While it was common courtesy to offer a stranger a drink of water, providing a drink for his camels and other animals represented an act of service and kindness. When Rebekah heard about the servant's situation, and that he needed to bring a wife home for Isaac, Rebekah offered to go and become Isaac's wife[30]. Once they were married, she loved Isaac and remained loyal to him, almost to a fault. She knew God promised Abraham that a great nation would be descended from him, and she also received her own message from God confirming that Jacob was going to be used in a very different way than Esau. Genesis 25:23 says:

The Lord said to her, "Two nations are in your womb, and two peoples from within you will be separated; one people will be stronger than the other, and the older will serve the younger."

When Rebekah heard this, she determined to give Jacob every opportunity to succeed, even if that meant favoring him over her other son. Genesis tells us that Isaac loved Esau and Rebekah loved Jacob[31], and that seemed to be a somewhat natural thing when you consider the personalities and characteristics of the two boys. Esau, the oldest, hunted and brought wild game for dad, while Jacob, the baby, quietly spent time at home with mom. It's easy to see how each parent could favor one boy or the other, but there was more to it in Rebekah's mind. Rebekah aspired to make sure Jacob received an inheritance, even if that meant being dishonest.

When Isaac grew old and was about to die, he sent Esau hunting for wild game to prepare him a meal to eat so that he could offer his blessing prior to his death. Receiving a father's blessing meant a great deal at this time in history. The blessing passed on from a father to a son imparted more than just a good luck wish and some advice, it passed on the family inheritance. This established the son's future as the next patriarch of the clan. Without the father's blessing, the son essentially became a servant to whomever received the blessing. Esau had already sacrificed his spiritual birthright as the oldest child in exchange for a bowl of soup because he lacked any true respect for the spiritual side of this blessing, but he knew all about the inheritance. So did Rebekah. When Esau eagerly left for his hunting trip, Rebekah and Jacob devised a plan for how they would trick Isaac. Jacob knew that Isaac had lost his sight, so all he had to do was wear some of Esau's clothing, put some animal hair on his arms so he felt like Esau, take Isaac some stew, and lie. Jacob, the heel grabber, the deceiver, the usurper, was doing what his mom told him to do[32].

The plan worked to perfection and Jacob became the next patriarch in the line of Abraham's family...exactly what God intended to happen. It's easy for us to look at Rebekah's actions and chastise her for being so dishonest. The deception of her husband and the split she caused between her sons affected their lives for years to come, but if anyone ever deserved a bit of grace, it was Rebekah. As I mentioned earlier, Rebekah was a loyal wife who loved Isaac. So loyal in fact that she didn't want him to make a mistake. She knew what

God had told her about Jacob being the blessed child, and she only wanted to help Isaac make the right decision. And just because she favored Jacob, didn't mean that she didn't love Esau as well. She didn't want to see him hurt, but she didn't want to stand idly by and not see God's plan come to fruition. There is much to be learned from Rebekah's determination and dedication, both good and bad. It's admirable to be so laser focused on what God has promised you and to go to great lengths to make sure that His kingdom is shepherded properly, but that can't be done without faith. While Rebekah possessed plenty of loyalty and determination, she lacked faith. She didn't trust God enough to simply let Him work out the situation on His own, but, once again, we see why God is so great. He doesn't need perfection; He only needs vessels. He knew how Rebekah would respond, and His plan moved ahead as scheduled. He also knew that Rebekah's loyalty and dedication to her family were traits that Jacob would see established in his own life because of her. Without his mother, Jacob would never have become the man that he ultimately became, and he may have let go of God altogether. God's plans may not always take the path that we think is obvious, but that's because His path is perfect.

~

Chapter 7
The God of Israel

~

Before we jump into this next section, I just want to acknowledge something. God's love for us is so great that He basically constructed a nation, piece by piece, from nothing. He took a pagan from Ur and said go, and Abraham obeyed. God blessed him with land, riches, and children. The next link was Isaac, and God blessed him and enlarged Isaac's riches to that greater than Abraham's. He built this family to be a big deal in the land of Canaan in just two generations. The king of the Philistines actually asked Isaac to leave the area because he had grown "too powerful".[33] God knew that in order to save the creation that He loved so much, He needed to establish a righteous bloodline, a bloodline capable of producing a righteous seed. So, He began placing people in positions to make this happen. He had established the foundation of this bloodline in Abraham and Isaac...and then there was Jacob.

What can we really say about Jacob other than "wow"? I mean, as we've discussed already, Jacob dealt a bit underhandedly with his family, but this didn't stop God. God appears to Jacob a few times after he tricks Isaac and Jacob eventually winds up at his uncle Laban's house where he marries Laban's daughters, Leah and Rachel. Jacob worked for Laban for almost twenty years, and in that time, his family and possessions grew. All in all, Jacob turned into a pretty powerful person in his own right.

One day, the Lord tells Jacob it was time to head back to his homeland, so Jacob goes. On his way, he stops to camp and decides to send some messengers to his brother, Esau, to let him know he's coming to see him. When the servants return, they tell Jacob that Esau was on his way to meet Jacob and had 400 men with him. Naturally, this concerns Jacob. Jacob had done a pretty horrible thing to Esau and is now worried that Esau is coming for revenge. Genesis says that Jacob experienced great fear and distress. He decides to divide everything he has into two groups because he figures that if Esau attacks one group, the other group can escape and at least he wouldn't lose everything[34]. Solid logic for sure, but we're talking about the grandson of Abraham here. Where is the faith? Jacob built his whole life on self-reliance. When we think back through the major events of his life, from deceiving Esau into selling him the spiritual birthright, working with his mother to trick Isaac into blessing him, growing more powerful than Laban using his own wit and intellect, and now working out a way to pacify Esau, we see a man, who recognized his own brilliance. It wasn't that Jacob didn't know who God was, or believe in God, he just didn't really have a relationship with God the way his father and grandfather did. He knows that God has blessed him, and he also knows that God has spoken to him, on several occasions, but Jacob still has not intimately experienced God in a way that makes him trust God, but all of that is about to change.

After sending gifts ahead with his servants and instructions on how to placate Esau, Jacob sends his family and all his possessions across the river. Jacob remains alone on the opposite side of the river. It's when we're alone that we really get an opportunity to encounter God. There are no distractions to rob us of our focus. It's almost impossible to be alone in today's world. Even when there are no other people around, we have computers, TVs, phones, and countless other distractions that keep us focusing on anything and everything, except God. Jacob didn't have these distractions. I've often thought about this moment as Jacob just sitting by a campfire worrying, maybe crying or even praying to the god of his father and grandfather, but not expecting much to come from any of it. It's in this alone time that God can begin to work some things out in us, and work things out is exactly what God did to Jacob once He was alone. Genesis 32:24 says:

So Jacob was left alone, and a man wrestled with him till daybreak.

I love the way this is written...there is no build up, there is no preparation, just bam...fight. I remember when I was a kid watching Saturday morning wrestling. I smile each time I think back to the character in the ring, brazenly addressing the crowd, always with his back to the place where the wrestlers enter the arena. There was never a doubt in his mind that he was the greatest. But then, out of nowhere, another wrestler enters the arena in a full sprint, dives into the ring with a metal folding chair, and SMASH...wrestling. Or maybe the one in the ring was a bit braggadocious in his reminders to the crowd how great he was when the other wrestlers intro music would all suddenly blast over the loudspeakers. The fear is unmistakable and the once confident man in the ring is now nothing more than terrified and confused, looking for any exit he can find, but there isn't one, because now it's time to wrestle. Can you imagine God's intro music? You're there, in the ring, alone, and you hear God's intro music, and you know who is coming to the ring.

I'm obviously drawing some pretty far-fetched comparisons here between Jacob wrestling God and two paid actors having a fake fight on a Saturday morning, but part of me honestly believes this is a bit of the way that God chose to get Jacob's attention. God didn't schedule this meeting in advance with Jacob, he waited until Jacob was rich and important. Jacob faced a problem and schemed a way to get out of it. Yeah, Jacob was still afraid and worried, but he also assumed the situation was under control. He might end up losing a little, but he was wealthy enough that it would be ok in the long run. He was pretty much thinking he could buy his way out of the problem. Then God showed up and smacked him with a metal folding chair. Jacob was alone...no one else, no distractions, just him, and that's all God needed.

The bible says that the man wrestled with Jacob and that when he realized he couldn't win he told Jacob to let him go, but he gives a reason. He says "let me go, for it is daybreak"[35]. Now, what does that really have to do with anything? I'm not really sure that God was concerned with it being light and someone seeing Jacob wrestling, but God knew that Jacob had to attend to his business. He had work to do, and the sun was coming up.

Jacob's evening spent wrestling with God marked the first time that Jacob intimately encountered God. While Jacob had heard God's voice and followed his directions, he had not truly been wrapped up in God in this manner. We spend a great deal of our days worrying about how to get things done. We have our own Esaus in our lives that we are trying to pacify. We have our own situations that require us to come up with quick witted resolutions or else we risk losing everything. We face situations in our lives that God has given us the ability to overcome, but he never intended for us to do it alone. Jacob took everything that night and laid it before God, and that's exactly what He wants each of us to do. God wants us to take every fear, every doubt, every concern, every worry, every infirmity, and lay it out in the ring. "Here it is God! This is what I've got. It's not good, but it's what I've got right now." It's this fervent prayer that is our wrestling match with God. When we reach a point that we are seeking Him with such relentless passion that we have no further concept of time and place is when we realize that the day is breaking. Daybreak means that it's time to go to work. Daybreak does not mean the job is done. Daybreak simply means that it's time to get the job done. It's at daybreak that we cry out, like Jacob did[36], "I won't let go until you bless me". We spend so much time in our prayer lives thinking that God's blessing means we don't have to face the day-to-day battles, but what it really means is that we don't have to face them alone, and this is the precise blessing that Jacob received.

Jacob's blessing is a bit of a strange one in the physical form. He received a new name and a limp. If ever there was a time that proved God's ways are not our own, it was this blessing. One of my favorite ways I consume God's word is to imagine being there myself knowing what I know now. I love to have these candid and casual conversations with God about how this must have looked and felt. Think about standing with God as Jacob is limping off and having a conversation.

"Ok God let's retrace this one if you don't mind. We've got a serious problem in the world because of what happened back in Eden. You created mankind, and they have pretty much turned evil, but you love them so much you're going to save them. Now, in order to save them, you've got this plan that will take a while (that's a whole different conversation with God we'll have a different time), but this guy Jacob is a pretty big piece of it. I know the guy has been a bit shifty for most of his life, but he just spent a night wrestling you, which is pretty impressive in its own right, and he wants a blessing. He's super persistent, super dedicated, and is imperative to your plan, so you rain down treasures from heaven in the form of a new name and limp?"

Now, all joking aside, I'm not suggesting that God is

some Three Stooges style contractor that is blundering through eternity and needs to be questioned. He's immensely Holy and His plans are perfect which is why I am always amazed when He chooses to reveal things to me in His word. I picture him standing there after I've asked my questions, watching Jacob limp away, a knowing smile on His face as he turns and winks and says, "watch this."

Jacob, whose new name is Israel, heads off to meet Esau. Much to Jacob's surprise, Esau is ecstatic to see him and rejoices that his baby brother has returned. Esau and Jacob actually argue a little over whether Esau should accept Jacob's gifts because he is just so pleased that Jacob is back. After the reunion, Jacob heads to Shechem in Canaan where he builds an altar and names it *El Elohe Israel*[37]. So why is this important? Why is this one line of scripture at the very end of a chapter in Genesis so telling? What does this one sentence do to prove how much God loves us? Well, in order to see that, we have to bounce back a few chapters. Genesis 28:13 says:

There above it stood the Lord, and he said: "I am the Lord, the God of your father Abraham and the God of Isaac. I will give you and your descendants the land on which you are lying.

Genesis 31:42 says:

If the God of my father, the God of Abraham and the Fear of Isaac, had not been with me, you would surely have sent me away empty-handed. But God has seen my hardship and the toil of my hands, and last night he rebuked you.

Genesis 32:9 says:

Then Jacob prayed, "O God of my father Abraham, God of my father Isaac, Lord, you who said to me, 'Go back to your country and your relatives, and I will make you prosper,'

Have you seen the pattern yet? I'll give you a hint, it's all about relationship. What does God want more than anything from us? Relationship. He wants us to be His. He wants us to know Him intimately, He wants us to be His children and He wants to be our father. When Jacob spent a night wrestling with God, he became acquainted with God in a way he had never been. He walked away with a permanent reminder that he, Jacob, the usurper and schemer, the shady character who had stolen his brother's blessings, was loved and chosen by God. He was no longer Jacob, the schemer, he was Israel, the father of a nation. And just like that, God was now El Elohe Israel, the God of Israel. He was no longer just the God that his father and grandfather knew. He was no longer the God that just blessed him because of the promises made to previous generations. God was his God.

Just when you reach the point that you begin to think that God's love is hidden is usually when the greatest reminders of how much He loves you show up. Jacob had every intention of spending a night alone, weeping and crying out to the God of his fathers for help, but he never expected what was coming. We spend our days filled with worry about things that are already handled. This knowledge doesn't mean that the worries magically go away, but it does mean that we are equipped with a solution. The solution requires work, though. It requires time and determination. It might require sleepless nights and tears. It might require anger and yelling. It might just require us to be still and alone for a while, but whatever it ends up requiring, it always results in God's presence. It may not erase every worry. Israel still had to get up and walk for hours and go meet Esau, but he was able to do it with the confidence that God was with him. He still questioned the outcome, and I'm sure he was still concerned, but now he had his God with him. When we reach a point that God is no longer a reference of whom someone speaks or a person from the Bible that we read about and gain inspiration we begin to walk with confidence. When we reach that place where we genuinely experience God's great love continuously being poured out on us, we begin to see things differently. We recognize that no fault or failure will ever keep us from that love. We grab hold of the words of Isaiah, and we see them become real and we know that no weapon formed against us will ever prosper[38] because the God of [Your Name] is bigger than any situation. And the God of [Your Name] loves [Your Name] more than you will ever truly be able to understand.

~

Part 3

Preparing For A King

~

Somewhere near the top of the mountain called Sinai, He sat, staring out at the horizon, His thoughts consumed with His Beloved. Day and night, He waited, longing for her to return to Him. He had diligently watched over her since the flood, never leaving her side, even though she seemed to take no notice. Dedicated to His Beloved, He remained steadfast and resolute in His plan to bring her back to Him for eternity. Oh, how He adored her. It made no difference to Him that she fell away, only that she returned. He would overlook an eternity of failures for her, because she was His Beloved, and nothing was more precious to him. Just then, His eye caught the faint glimmer on the horizon and a smile crossed his face as He began to make out her silhouette. It was her, His Beloved! "Soon, My Love", He said aloud though almost inaudibly. "The seed has been planted."

~

Chapter 8
Chosen Imperfections

~

What exactly does it mean to be chosen? When we think of the word chosen, most of the time we think that we've been picked or selected for something. But there is a little more to it that we don't often realize. To be chosen, selected, or picked for something means that there is some sort of intrinsic value offered by "the chosen". If I am putting together a team for a softball game, the people that I choose to be on the team are those who offer me the best opportunity to win. When I'm choosing my team, I'm looking for value and what the ones I choose can offer me. Isn't it so perfectly wonderful that our God doesn't choose us based on what we can offer him?! We are chosen simply because He loves us...nothing more. If nothing else is learned of God's love from the great heroes of the Bible that we've discussed thus far, Adam, Noah, Abraham, Isaac, and Jacob, and even more so from the ones we will look at in the coming pages we've seen that God's love does not require us to earn it. As the prophet Isaiah put it, "all our righteous acts are like filthy rags"[39], yet He still loves us more than anything.

There is, perhaps, no greater example of God's unfailing love in the face of epic failure than that of the Israelites. The nation of Israel was descended from Abraham. That fulfilment of God's promise to the patriarch of His mighty plan to redeem the human race that He loved so much. These were the offspring of the twelve sons of Jacob, chosen specifically to produce a righteous Messiah to save us all. With that type of purpose, it would seem that this would be a group that had it together. And if nothing else, you would think that the Israelites at least had some pride about their meaning on earth and what they were to accomplish. The truth is most of them had no clue about any promised savior. Throughout the Old Testament, and sadly, even now, so many people missed the message of Christ. The Old Testament is full of promises of the coming Messiah and reminders that the Nation of Israel were the people chosen to usher the Messiah into the world. Yet sadly, these messages fell on more deaf ears than hearing. God's unending love for His creation had to be big enough to overcome an entire world's worth of rejection and indifference, on multiple occasions. Luckily for us, it was, and it is.

God's plan to save the people that so easily rejected Him was amazing in so many ways, but perhaps none greater than that, while using so many people, it relied on none of them. The idea that we are to be vessels used by God to pour out His amazing love on those who don't yet know that love is written on almost every page in the Bible. God plan perfectly uses imperfect humans as the main part of the plan to spread a perfect love.

One of my favorite examples of this perfect use of imperfection is found in Deuteronomy 18. Seemingly out of nowhere, Moses transitions from explaining different stipulations surrounding the Levitical priests to mentioning a promise that God had made. Deuteronomy 18:15 says:

The Lord your God will raise up for you a prophet like me from among you, from your fellow Israelites. You must listen to him.

"A prophet like me..."? Like Moses? What characteristics did Moses possess exactly that God wanted to use? The stuttering? The temper? The doubt? Moses wasn't exactly the mild-mannered man that we see depicted in the cartoon movies. He feared God, but he wasn't perfect. Moses makes a reference later in this same chapter that explains exactly why God wanted to raise up a prophet like Moses. Moses' words take the people all the way back to Mt Sinai...back to when they were chosen.

~

Exodus 19 is an incredible display of the presence of God and illustrates one of my all-time favorite reactions to his presence. I love to read about Isaiah when he saw the Lord and "his train filled the temple[40], or Revelation when the angel shows John the throne room of God with the 24 elders falling on their faces and worshipping the Almighty[41]. I love to read these encounters because we are so guilty of forgetting how truly Holy and incredible our God is. This grand love that He offers us is only possible because of his immense holiness. If our God was not so great that all creation knelt before Him and sang "Holy, Holy, Holy, is the Lord God Almighty, who was, and is, and is to come!" over and over and over again, He would never have been able to redeem us from life without Him.

Like Isaiah and John, the Israelites were being prepared to get a glimpse of something incredible. The sequence of events that had taken place over the past 30 days for the Israelites had been pretty intense. Prior to actually leaving Egypt, they witnessed some awesome things, and now, God wanted to show them something even greater...Himself. When the Israelites arrived at Mt Sinai, Moses provided instructions for how to prepare themselves. They had to consecrate themselves so that they could be in the presence of God. Consecration was serious business, and everyone knew it, but no one understood exactly how serious until the presence of God descended on Mt Sinai. As God rained down His presence before the Israelites the Bible says that there was thunder and lightning, smoke covered the mountain, and the whole mountain shook. It also says that every person trembled[42]. You may be wondering to yourself, "What's so awesome about all of them trembling?". Yes, obviously the power of the presence of God was awesome to behold, but there is something even better here...the knowledge that they were in the presence of God. At this one moment, perhaps the only moment in history since God created mankind, everyone near Sinai knew exactly what they were experiencing. Each person whom God had chosen to be "His people" stood, in reverent fear, of the Almighty God. At this very moment, a unity unlike anything prior or sense existed. What an awesome experience it must have been at that moment.

I want to make sure I express this clearly because it's

such an amazing concept that we miss so many times. Our time together thus far has been spent looking at the great love of our mighty God - A love so intense that we haven't yet been able to define, explain, grasp, or comprehend. But we can't define, explain, grasp, or comprehend our God either. Coincidence? Nope. We can't wrap our brains around either separately because they're not separate. God is love! Our God is LOVE! HE IS LOVE!! We can't escape this mind-blowing love that He has for us because we can't escape Him. There is never a time that we can be in His presence and not experience His love. At the base of Mt Sinai, this wonderful and perfect love immersed Israel...and each person knew it! What happens next is my favorite part. Moses comes down off of the mountain and the Israelites look at him and basically tell him that they can't handle this anymore. They saw the immense and raw power of their God and they knew that He was something a lot more than they were ready for. They tell Moses in Exodus 20:18:

Speak to us yourself and we will listen. But do not have God speak to us or we will die.

They knew of their unworthiness to be in the presence of such an amazing power and they were afraid. We hate to think of God as something that we should fear, but that's because we don't want to acknowledge the power of God. We want to think about the great love of the father, but we don't want to recognize the hatred of sin. But we have something the Israelites didn't have - Christ. When Christ died for us, we were given an all-access pass into the throne room of God because His blood took away our guilt. While the Israelites realized at this moment that they weren't worthy, we recognize that we are worthy, because Christ made us worthy. It's because of Christ that we can exist in the presence of God.

After the nation of Israel has experienced God's presence, God called Moses up onto Mt Sinai. Moses spends a long time up there with God while God gives him all sorts of instructions. While Moses is gone, the people grow restless and totally ignore everything they had just experienced. They approach Aaron and tell him to build them a god that they can see[43]. Every time I read this passage, I just shake my head, for two reasons. One, they had just experienced the Creator of the Universe up close and personal - So up close and personal that they told Moses to stand between them. The God they are supposed to be serving just introduced Himself in a way that blew their minds! So why did they ask for a god they could see? Because the god they could see wouldn't make the mountains quake. When the mountains tremble and smoke it's scary.

The second reason the golden calf upsets me so much is that we're no different. How many times have you prayed for God to do something awesome in your life, only to spin around and ignore Him? Have you ever said "God, I just need you to show up in my life like you never have before" and then sat down on the couch and forgot about Him for the rest of the night? We pray for mighty acts of God, but the truth is, we're terrified of them actually happening because it might just wreck our little world we've created for ourselves. The golden calf sits quietly on the mantle and doesn't do anything, EVER, but we can see him...we tell ourselves he's there for us. We allow the false hope of a false god to control our lives because we think it's safe. Sure, you're probably not sitting in your living room kneeling before a shrine of a golden calf, but you are worshipping something other than the God that loves you so much that He will shake a mountain to make you see it. You think I'm not talking about you in this too? When was the last time you turned off the TV, the cell phones, the laptops, or whatever else you have that takes your attention away from the Almighty and cried out to Him for your family, or your job, or whatever situation you're facing? When was the last time that you stopped criticizing the programs and the leaders in the church and started weeping for the people that are attending that church? When was the last time that you asked God to forgive you and everyone else because we are more concerned with our comfortable and easy life than we are with the people that He loves so much? When was the last time you stopped worshipping yourself and worshipped El Shaddai?

God was willing to use Moses as a template because Moses was willing to put others before himself. While the Israelites reveled in their worship of the golden calf, God tells Moses to tend to the situation, and God is angry. Moses addresses the people and then returns to God, then he does something amazing. Exodus 32:31-32 say:

So Moses went back to the Lord and said, "Oh, what a great sin these people have committed! They have made themselves gods of gold. But now, please forgive their sin – but if not, then blot me out of the book you have written.

Moses was willing to be the sacrifice for the people. Moses didn't tell God that he wasn't involved. He didn't run back up to the top of Sinai and say "God, I was right here with you the whole time. I wasn't part of that. I didn't make that mess." He asked God to wipe him out if it meant that they would get another chance. This is the love that God wants us to have for His children and this is why God promised to raise up a prophet like Moses. God isn't worried about our abilities and imperfections; He just wants our hearts. He wants us to be heartbroken because someone isn't hearing about His unfailing love and is risking an eternity apart from Him. He wants us to seek opportunities to spread the word of His Kingdom so that no one will miss out. He wants us to be like Nehemiah when he returned and saw Jerusalem in ruins. Nehemiah fell down and wept because God's city had been destroyed. His heart broke because he witnessed the ruin and destruction, not just of the city, but of the people[44]. When was the last time our hearts were broken for the destruction of God's church and His people? When was the last time we shared the heart of God?

We hide behind our imperfections every day. We say things like "I'm too busy" or "I'm not qualified" or "I'm not dealing with that headache". The imperfections in our lives tend to be excuses, more than actual problems. We don't want to acknowledge that God can use us to shake a mountain because that means we have to address our own selfishness. Thankfully, God doesn't need us to address anything, He will happily address these imperfections for us, because all He needs is one person to genuinely care...one person to really love His people...one person to cry out, heart-broken for the lost sheep. All He needs is one imperfect person. He built an entire nation from the faith of one imperfect person. Imagine what He could do with the faith of an entire generation of people who trusted Him with their imperfections.

~
Chapter 9
Give Us A King
~

When we look at what God has done for us throughout history, we see this incredible love that could only come from Him. There's no way any of us could love something the way He has loved us. There's no way any of us could sacrifice for anything, or anyone, the way He has for us. When we look at this love, it warms our hearts that our creator cares so much for us that He was willing to go through all He went through just so that we could be near Him. But we don't ever recognize that God got angry too. There were several times over the course of His plan to rescue His beloved creation that He got mad and let Israel's enemies overtake them. We'll talk about more of the details later, but even during the times that God got angry he was still demonstrating His love for us. He loved us, and cared enough, to get mad on occasion. If He didn't love us, He would have just thrown His hands up and walked away, leaving us to an eternity separated from Him. When we love something, we are passionate about it. And when we are passionate about something, we can get angry at it. Anger is not a sin; it's how we handle our anger that can potentially cause problems.

When we think about God's anger, we tend to immediately jump to events in the Bible like the Flood, the destruction of Sodom and Gomorrah, or the captivity of Israel and Judah by Assyria and Babylon. God's anger was definitely displayed in these instances, but there is one huge example of God's anger that I think often flies under our radar. In the eighth chapter of 1st Samuel, Samuel grows old and nears the end of his life. Samuel was the last Judge of Israel. If you recall, after the death of Joshua, Israel was ruled by Judges, some good, some bad, but all appointed by God. Over the course of a few hundred years, 14 judges led the Israelites, ending with the prophet Samuel. The book of Judges, chapter two tells us that after Joshua's generation had passed away, another generation that didn't know God or what He had done for the Israelites rose to take their place[45]. Israel had more than fallen away from their God, they had completely abandoned everything that He had told them to do. That's not to say that some righteous men and women didn't exist in Israel, but at this time in history, consistency was non-existent.

As Samuel neared the end of his life, he appointed his sons as leaders of Israel. This decision was not well received by the people because, much like his predecessor Eli, Samuel had some pretty terrible sons. They were priests who abused their power for selfish gain, and the people were not big fans of this decision. The elders of Israel came to Samuel and told him that they wanted a king. To be specific, they said (1 Sam 8:5):

You are old, and your sons do not follow your ways; now appoint a king to lead us, such as all the other nations have.

Now, most anyone who has studied God's word a little recognizes this request as a bad thing. We know that the king they got was Saul and that he wasn't a great guy. If they had trusted God and followed Him, they wouldn't even need a king, right? Well, kind of. The truth is, God had already told the Israelites that He would give them a king. Deuteronomy 17:14-20 outline God's requirements for a king:

When you come to the land that the Lord your God is giving you, and you possess it and dwell in it and then say, 'I will set a king over me, like all the nations that are around me,' you may indeed set a king over you whom the Lord your God will choose. One from among your brothers you shall set as king over you. You may not put a foreigner over you, who is not your brother. Only he must not acquire many horses for himself or cause the people to return to Egypt in order to acquire many horses, since the Lord has said to you, 'You shall never return that way again.' And he shall not acquire many wives for himself, lest his heart turn away, nor shall he acquire for himself excessive silver and gold. "And when he sits on the throne of his kingdom, he shall write for himself in a book a copy of this law, approved by the Levitical priests. And it shall be with him, and he shall read in it all the days of his life, that he may learn to fear the Lord his God by keeping all the words of this law and these statutes, and doing them, that his heart may not be lifted up above his brothers, and that he may not turn aside from the commandment, either to the right hand or to the left, so that he may continue long in his kingdom, he and his children, in Israel.

God laid out several requirements for Israel's future king. The king had to be chosen by the Lord, must be an Israelite, must not acquire many horses for himself, must not have too many wives, gold, or silver, and he must have a copy of the law with him to study. These seem to be fairly reasonable requests. Basically, God is saying he was going to pick someone to be the king who was one of His chosen people, who was humble and would rely on Him, and would study His word so that he knows how to follow God. Easy right? So, if God laid all of this out for the Israelites, why was their request for a king such a bad idea? 1 Sam 8:7-8 says:

And the Lord told him: "Listen to all that the people are saying to you; it is not you they have rejected, but they have rejected me as their king. As they have done from the day I brought them up out of Egypt until this day, forsaking me and serving other gods, so they are doing to you.

God wasn't worried about the king; He had already told them they would have a king. He was upset because they didn't recognize Him as their king. They were looking for a man to take on the role of the king that they saw in the surrounding countries. Kings that would go into battle first and be the great champion of the people. Kings that provided for their subjects and make sure their needs were met. Kings were the ultimate leader by example, and what better king to have than the King of Kings! God had countless times gone into battle ahead of the nation of Israel and given them victory. He had provided miraculously for them over and over since their inception. Yet, no one remembered this, no one cared. They wanted a king

that they could see and compare to other nations. Does
this behavior remind you of a certain request to make a
golden calf? It should, because the motive behind
Israel's request for a king was the same as the motive
behind asking Aaron to create the golden calf. Israel
looked for something they could see, touch, and feel.
They wanted something that didn't require faith to
believe in.

God's response was, frankly, scary. God tells Samuel
to give them a king but to make sure that he explained
exactly what the king would do to them. Samuel tells
the Israelites about all of the oppression that they
would feel under a king[46], everything from having to
pay the king a tenth of their harvest to their sons being
put to work as fieldhands and soldiers. Having a
physical king that didn't line up with what God laid
out in Deuteronomy meant oppression for the
Israelites, but the worst part of having the king came in
verse 18. 1 Samuel 8:18 says:

When that day comes, you will cry out for relief from the
king you have chosen, but the Lord will not answer you in
that day.

God's love for His creation was tested again on this
day. The wonderful love of our father was held to
flames, so to speak, and luckily, it didn't catch fire.
God knew that this was going to happen, and while he
was angry and determined to let Israel suffer some, He
still knew His plan was right on track. The king that
God had described for the Israelites in Deuteronomy
was His son, Christ. He knew that Israel would one

day have a king that was holy and just and would reign over His people in an upright way. He would love His people and provide for them, take care of them, and sustain them. He would guide them in godly ways. God knew mankind could never live up to His standards. Saul selfishly focused on his glory and not God's. David committed adultery, murderer, and craved power. Solomon had tons or horses and wives and married an Egyptian princess, and the list of Israelites (and Judean) kings goes on and on and on with similar, and worse, faults. That's not to say that these men didn't have good qualities. Saul was charismatic and a good leader. He made Israel a powerful nation. David was a man after God's own heart because he recognized his weaknesses and repented for them constantly, seeking God's will in His life and kingdom. Solomon chose godly wisdom over any other gift in the world. God used these men, who would never be able to live up to His standards for a king, to further His plan of redemption for the human race. He used these earthly kings to continue to establish the bloodline that would eventually produce the Messiah. The Messiah that would save our entire race from certain death.

God's anger is just one more area where, we can find His immense love for us. It's this anger that reminds us that He loves us enough to be upset when we're doing something that doesn't line up with His plan for us. God's very first commandment to Moses on Mt Sinai was that there were to be no other gods but Him[47]. God didn't give this command because He had an ego. He gave it because He knew what was best for us. Part of being God is knowing everything, including the fact that He is God. God knows exactly who He is. He knows He is holy; He knows He is all powerful, He knows that His way is the best way to get us through life, and He knows that without Him, we don't stand a chance. He knows all of these things because He is God. He doesn't tell us that we can only worship Him because He needs the attention. He tells us that we can only worship Him because He knows that without Him, we're not going to make it. If we're worshipping other things, that worship would only lead to death, and when we disobey, there are consequences. He doesn't get angry in the way that we do. There is no sin in His anger. God never has to come back to us and apologize for being mad. His anger is righteous and based in love, and without it, we would be cursed to an eternity apart from Him with no chance of salvation.

~

Chapter 10
The Good Shepherd

~

God's anointing is a wonderful thing. When we think about God's anointing, we tend to think of priests and kings. And while that is technically who was anointed, there was more to the practice of anointing than we generally acknowledge. The word anoint actually means to smear or rub with oil and took place almost daily in the lives of the Israelites. There were two very different types of anointing. There was God's anointing, that used the anointing oil God instructed Moses how to make in Exodus,[48] and this is what we typically think about when we think of anointing. Another type of anointing, although less festive, happened daily. The anointings occurred for very different reasons, but as we are about to learn, they parallel each other remarkably. Isn't it amazing that we serve a God that can take something, or someone (you...I'm talking about you) that is common and make them holy!

I think most of us are all familiar with Psalms 23. David's "Shepherd's Psalm" is one of the most famous passages in all of the Bible, and I've always loved it because of the comfort that it brings. It's an awesome example of true trust in our God. But why does it comfort me? In truth, because I memorized it when I was about 7 years old, and someone told me it was comforting. Don't roll your eyes at that! I promise you that you're holding onto some habits, or rhetoric, or something that you heard someone else tell you once and never really questioned. And you know what, that's ok. Just because someone told me that Psalm 23 was a Psalm of encouragement and comfort didn't make it any less encouraging and comforting when I needed it to be. God doesn't need us to be scholars, He wants us to believe in Him. We can't understand all of His ways, and He doesn't expect us to, He just wants us to trust Him. There, you got that one for free...now back to Psalm 23.

Now, before we look at this chapter, I need you to get one thing into your mind right now. This is important in order for us to go any further with this: You are a sheep. In this chapter, Psalm 23, you are a sheep (or a lamb, whichever you prefer right now) and the Lord is your shepherd. I'm not just being mean here. It's important to realize the context of this psalm because it's only then that we can begin to get a glimpse of what David was talking about. So, you're a sheep, and you're hanging out in the green pastures and being led beside the still waters. The Lord is your shepherd, right? Life is good. The fact that the Lord is our shepherd makes life wonderful, but let me throw something out at you, being a sheep isn't all it's cracked up to be. Sheep are stupid animals. They'll follow the flock wherever the flock goes. There are tons of stories of flocks of sheep walking off of cliffs because one sheep fell off. They just follow each other blindly. Wherever the flock goes, so goes the individual sheep. You know what else sheep are? Stubborn! Ouch, that one kind of hit me too...maybe I'll delete that part later so I don't convict myself. Sheep are also needy. They can't just do things for themselves; they have to be shown everything. The shepherd had to show them where the water was, show them where the green grass was, make sure they didn't wander off into dangerous ground, and so much more. As bad as it was to be a sheep, being a shepherd was worse.

In the days that David wrote this Psalm, being a shepherd was a seriously dangerous gig. David didn't just hang out in the meadow, play the guitar and write songs while the little lambs frolicked around him. No, David was in the wilderness with the wild animals, and the thorns, and the rocks, and every other danger you can imagine. He was alone with the sheep, and it was up to him to ensure their wellbeing. Providing for sheep started when they were young. Remember how I said that sheep would follow the flock blindly? Well, to combat this, shepherds would begin training the lambs to follow them when the lambs were young. I'm about to rock your world, so hold on. Remember the picture in your Sunday School class when you were younger, of Jesus holding the little lamb on His shoulders? The wonderful shepherd holding the cute little lamb? Yeah, you remember. You're remembering it right now. You can see it in your mind. Do you see the broken leg on the lamb? Seriously? Do you see it? No, you don't see it because it wasn't there. The image didn't show that part of what was going on. You see, when a lamb was particularly stubborn and wouldn't follow the shepherd, the shepherd would take his rod and break the little lamb's leg. Now the little lamb couldn't walk away and had to be carried by the shepherd. The lamb was in pain and had to rely on the shepherd constantly for everything, or he would die. He depended on the shepherd for food, water, transportation, protection, and everything else. There was nothing the little lamb could do without the shepherd, but by the time the leg healed, the little lamb trusted the shepherd completely, and followed him without question or delay. This is the essence of Psalm 23. The Lord is my shepherd, I have everything I need[49].

As we look at the following verses in Psalm 23, we see the life of a shepherd really unfold before us. The shepherd makes the sheep lie down in green pastures[50]. How peaceful and serene, right? Actually, when sheep were wandering around in the pastures, they would get cuts and the sores that would get infected. In order to save the sheep, the shepherd would force the sheep to lie down in the pasture while he cut the sores out and treated them. If the sheep was left to wander around, never being treated for the things that were causing it pain, never having the infections cut out of them, they would eventually just die. It's the shepherd's job to force the sheep to lie down and cut out the bad. It's not pleasant, for the sheep or the shepherd, but where would we be if our shepherd didn't love us enough to work on us like this.

What about the next line, being led beside still waters[51]? Have you ever stood on the banks of a big river with rapids? It's not quiet. The crashing water working its way over the rocks makes a wonderfully loud sound. It's also fast. I took my boys fishing awhile back on the banks of a local river and as one of them leaned over to put his hand in the water, I casually stepped closer to him, just in case he tipped too far, so I could get him before the water swept him away. These are the same reasons the shepherd leads his sheep beside still waters. Remember earlier when I said that sheep were stupid? The shepherd couldn't lead the sheep beside the fast-flowing river. The sheep would either get scared of the noise or they would fall in and get swept away in the fast-flowing current. God knows that we need the still waters. We need the quiet, non-distracting, safe waters that only the good shepherd can find. It's these waters that allow us to refocus and refresh. It's these waters that allow us to keep healing from our time in the pastures when we were made to lie down.

As we keep moving through Psalm 23, we see the shepherd leading his sheep on the safe path[52]. The shepherd knows the dangers that are present as he moves his flock from pasture to pasture, and he also knows which paths are safest. And then there is the dark valley. We all know the verse, Psalm 23:4:

Even though I walk through the darkest valley, I will fear no evil, for you are with me; your rod and your staff, they comfort me[53].

So much about this single verse shows us how much God loves us. Remember when the shepherd broke the little lamb's leg? How terrible it must have felt for the shepherd, to take his rod and break that little lamb's leg. Can you imagine the cries of pain from the little lamb? The look of terror on the little lamb's face, not realizing that the shepherd was doing this for his own good. The Shepherd, broken hearted, could only watch as the little lamb tried to get away from what he thought was his enemy. The little lamb simply didn't understand what was happening. But now, that little lamb is a sheep, who sees his shepherd ahead of him carrying his staff. The same staff that once caused the little lamb pain is now providing safety and comfort. The sheep knows the shepherd won't allow anything to hurt it. The shepherd will lead it to the place of safety and nourishment. No dark valley, no wild animal, no enemy can hurt the sheep as long as the shepherd is there.

So now we finally make our way to the anointing. He anoints my head with oil[54]. Why does he anoint my head with oil if I'm just a sheep? Well, there are a couple different things we can examine here - the first being the general shift in David's writing. The line prior to this tells us that God prepares a table before us in the presence of our enemies[55]. Since when did sheep start sitting at tables? David takes a pretty significant turn at this point in his writing that steps away from the sheep analogy. We've looked at the first four verses from the perspective of the sheep, and David is very obvious in his writing that he is the sheep. Sheep are dumb, stubborn, dependent on the shepherd, skittish, and afraid. Sheep are immature in their faith. Sheep are young in their understanding and lacking in their ability to trust in God. Sheep need the shepherd to provide for them, but in verse five, David suddenly shifts from sheep to faithful follower of God. He stands and declares that his God is big enough to prepare a table for him right in front of his enemies. Have you ever really thought about this? You're in battle and God sets the table and says to eat. But what about the enemies? Hate to break it to you, but they're at the table too. They're staring at you, whispering to you, taunting you. But you don't have to listen because God has set this table, and He is bigger than the enemy on the other side. You're sitting at the table prepared by the master. You're His prized possession. All you have to do is eat and trust.

As David continues, he drifts further away from the sheep analogy. The word anoint used in Psalm 23:5 is a very different word than what is used in other passages. The Hebrew word for anoint is MASHACH, which literally means to rub or smear with oil. We already established this right? Well, that's not what David wrote. The word David used was DISHANTA, which means to fatten or make healthy. Basically, David said you make my head fat. Doesn't quite have the same ring to it, does it? What the verse is saying is that God prepared this table for David in the presence of all his enemies and gave him the confidence to stand before them, believing God was with him. The fattened head was David's ego of sorts. Not a bad ego, but an insistent belief that his God was bigger than any problem that could come his way.

So, if God didn't actually anoint his head with oil, why did we translate it that way? That brings me to my next point of why David's writing was translated the way it was. There is always the possibility that maybe the translators just got it wrong. Or maybe the Hebrew dictionaries that we use now to translate the English are wrong? Or maybe the English translation of the Hebrew is incorrect which leads us to looking up the wrong word in Hebrew which makes us wrong. Or, and here is my personal belief, don't you think it's possible that it's translated exactly the way God intended for it to be translated? God knew exactly what David meant. He knew exactly what the next person that copied David's words meant. He knew exactly what the first published Bible was going to say. He knew exactly what you memorized when you were a kid, and He knew exactly what I was going to write today. God knows exactly what is happening and His plan will never fail, no matter how something may be translated. So, when the Bible says that God anoints my head with oil, then I'm lean in and expect the oil flow.

Well then, does that make us sheep or not? I don't think we will ever have days when we're not sheep, no matter how mature in our faith we are. No matter how much we grow, the shepherd will have to hold us down and cut some bad out of us at some point. No matter how much we trust, there will be days when we fail. So, with that in mind, let's be sheep again for a few more minutes to understand this anointing. When David was a shepherd, he had to anoint his sheep with oil almost daily for a couple of different reasons. First, sheep were a bit messy, which attracted flies and other bugs. The flies would find their way into the sheep's ears and lay eggs in the sheep's brain. This was painful and the sheep would actually ram its head against rocks to try and stop the pain, eventually cracking its own skull. The oil on the sheep's head was a way to keep the flies from being able to crawl around on the sheep. The second reason was to keep sheep from hurting themselves when they butt heads with each other. Sheep, when they were all together in the flock, would find themselves in conflict or competition with other sheep and would butt their heads together. This would inevitably lead to injuries, and in some cases death. The oil on the sheep's head would cause them to slide off of the other sheep without causing as much damage.

When our shepherd decides to anoint us with oil, he is doing it so that we are safe and protected. We are surrounded by evil every day. Each of our senses is constantly assaulted by a barrage of sin at every moment of the day. Short of locking yourself away in a closet, it's impossible to escape the immorality that exists in today's world. Enter the shepherd with his oil. The oil that our God pours on our heads each day is what helps keep the flies out. It keeps us from allowing the evil to penetrate our brains and destroy us from within.

Likewise, this oil keeps us from hurting ourselves and other believers. Conflict is going to happen, and can be healthy, but when we are in conflict without the anointing, that conflict can only end in death. The oil allows our human nature to glance off of each other and not cause serious spiritual damage. It's the oil of the shepherd that keeps us from hurting ourselves and our fellow believers.

God's love for us is an amazing parallel of the good shepherd. David's Psalm is a reminder to each of us of how much God loves us and the lengths that He goes to for each and every one of us. It's this example of God's love that reminds us that He never gives up on His beloved and that He will never forsake us. He put His wonderful plan into action years prior to David writing his Shepherd's Psalm, and He knew that David was going to be singing this praise to Him years later. He also knew that there was coming a time when we would dwell in the house of the Lord, forever[56].

~

Chapter 11
Anointed To Wait

~

D.L. Moody once said, *There is no use in running before you are sent; there is no use in attempting to do God's work without God's power. A man working without this unction, a man working without this anointing, a man working without the Holy Ghost upon him, is losing time after all.*

I love this quote. It sums up the importance of God's involvement in our lives in such a perfect way. Think about all that we have seen thus far on this trip from creation. No part of any of the actions of any of the people that God has used suggests, even for a moment, that God wasn't completely in control. Not a single one. Sure, these men and women weren't perfect, but God had determined to use them for His cause and nothing that they could have done would have changed that. No matter how many times we fail, God's anointing never will.

No man in the Bible, in my opinion, exemplifies Moody's quote more than David. I'm not talking about King David either, I'm talking about shepherd David, musician David, giant killer David, fugitive David, depressed David, scared David, humble David...I can keep going but I think you get the point. David, one of the greatest heroes in the Bible, was a man after God's own heart. However, David wasn't born a hero. David wasn't born an anointed king or a giant killer either. David was born the youngest son of a farmer and once he was old enough, he was sent to tend his father's sheep. The job of shepherd tended to be boring, lonely, and difficult and was generally reserved for the youngest son or for a servant. Sheep were a large source of the family's status and livelihood so making sure they were taken care of was important. Losing a sheep was unacceptable. The shepherd defended the flock against predators and thieves as well as tended to the overall health and wellbeing of the flock. David grew up pretty quickly in order to make sure his father's sheep, and himself, were safe.

David spent a lot of time alone in the fields with the sheep. He spent most of his time devoid of human company, so he began to do something that ended up molding his entire life...he prayed. Whether David was talking, singing, playing a harp, or whatever other form it may have taken, he was interacting with God. He made God his friend during these times. He sang praises to Him, talked with Him, consulted Him, and trusted Him. The relationship that David established with God became the foundation for everything else that David would accomplish in his life, and more importantly, it was the foundation that kept him from self-destruction. This time alone in the fields made David a man after God's own heart.

While David tended his father's sheep and grew closer to God, the anointed King of Israel was heading in the other direction. Saul, the first king of Israel, was anointed by God to do great things. After God told Samuel to anoint Saul as king, Samuel gave Saul a few brief instructions and then told him to do whatever he wanted, because God was with him[57]. Make no mistake about it, God ordained Saul to be the king of Israel and God did not make a mistake. Saul did a lot of good things for the nation of Israel. He united the tribes into a unified nation and established Israel as a military force by creating the infrastructure that would eventually lead to the creation of a powerful army. Saul, though he started out pretty timid, was a good king in human eyes. He won battles and made sacrifices to God and the people of Israel rallied behind him. However, the most important thing that Saul did as king was to unintentionally create an environment that would eventually force David to rely on God in unimaginable ways.

One day David was tending his father's sheep, just like normal, when a messenger showed up and told him that his father had summoned him home. David rushed home and found his father and Samuel, the prophet, waiting for him. Samuel anointed David and David returned back to the sheep[58]. Really kind of anticlimactic isn't it? I mean, consider how David must have felt. The youngest brother, picked on and relegated to the job of shepherd his entire life, is now being anointed to be king by the prophet Samuel. His brothers must have been amazed. David must have been amazed. David didn't know why he had been summoned home and suddenly he was told that he was God's anointed and going to be king. Oh, and by the way, get back to the sheep. That's got to sting. What was David thinking about on his way back to the pastures? What was he considering about the strange set of events that had just taken place? Was he the king or not? The answer he soon realized was no, he was not. He was anointed, but he was not the king. That job was still Saul's.

~

So now we have David, the anointed future king of Israel, in the fields tending sheep when a messenger again showed up and told him he needed to report to the palace. Saul, who God had rejected as king due to his disobedience[59], suffered from an evil tormenting spirit[60] and his servants told him that he needed to find a skilled musician to soothe him. Saul asked around, heard about David and sent for him. David was finally on his way to the palace, but not to be king, to be a servant. David willingly engaged in whatever Saul asked him to do and Saul began to really like David. Saul appointed David as one of his armor bearers and told his father Jesse that he was pleased with David and requested that Jesse allow David to stay. David remained in the service of Saul but returned to his father to help with the sheep on occasion. What a strange way to begin your time as God's anointed, splitting time between being a servant at the palace that you will one day rule, and a field tending to your father's sheep. It wouldn't have been a huge surprise if David had developed a bad attitude over all of this, but he didn't, he remained faithful and continued to do both of his lowly jobs with honor.

David had been performing double duty for a while and then there was a war between the Israelites and the Philistines that began. You know the story of David and Goliath, but it's an important piece of David's development so hang on. At this time in history, armies gathered on opposite sides of a big valley and stared at each other. Neither army would attack because that meant going down into the valley, giving the other army the high ground, so they just stood there and sent out a champion. Each army would send their champion and whoever emerged victorious claimed victory for their side. The Philistines loved this because they had Goliath. Goliath was a big dude. He was over nine feet tall, his armor weighed about 125 pounds, and the point of his spear weighed close to 15 pounds[61]. That's a lot of champion. The Israelites saw Goliath and were afraid, Saul included. The bible says that Saul was "a head taller than everyone else"[62], meaning he was bigger than the rest of the Israelites. He was also the king. The king was the protector and leader of the nation. The king was supposed to lead the men into battle. The king was the champion! But Saul was afraid. He wouldn't face Goliath because he saw his size and didn't want any part of him. Goliath taunted the Israelite army for 40 days, utterly destroying any moral that existed in their camp.

Meanwhile, David was in Bethlehem tending the sheep again and his father summoned him and told him to take some food to the battle lines for his brothers and see how they were doing[63]. David took everything to the battlefield where he heard Goliath taunting. David, infuriated, marched into Saul's tent and told him he would handle Goliath and Saul obliges. David descended into the valley, hit Goliath with a rock from his sling, and then used Goliath's sword to cut his head off. Easy right? When you're God's anointed and you have faith like David did, yes, easy. David was now a permanent fixture at the palace and Saul gave him a pretty high military rank as a reward. Anything that Saul asked him to do, David did it successfully[64]. It seemed that Saul and David both had a pretty good thing going, but then something happened that changed everything and set the course for years of suffering for both men.

One day, while Saul and David were returning from battle, a group of women came out and began singing, "Saul has slain his thousands, but David his tens of thousands."[65] This one line, one single line from a song, wrecked everything for Saul and David. When Saul heard the song, he was furious. Jealousy swarmed him and he suddenly hated David. He was terrified that David was plotting to take his kingdom and his hatred for David grew with each passing day. Saul despised David so much that he randomly threw spears at David in an attempt to pin him to the wall and kill him. David, however, continued to serve Saul faithfully, and even though Saul slung spears at him on almost a daily basis, David just dodged them and continued his duties. Dodging spears is a great talent to have, but the real testament to your faith in God is what you do after you dodge the spear. David never threw a spear back. He never stockpiled the spears for a future attack or to prevent Saul from one. No, he simply continued serving and dodging. The truth is, once you have dodged one spear, there are probably more coming, so be ready.

As David and Saul's relationship continued to deteriorate, it became evident that David could no longer remain in the palace if he wanted to live. But wait, David was anointed to be the king of Israel, right? If God told David that he would be the king, why was David running? David ran because a mad king was throwing spears at him. Faith in God or not, that's something worth running from. It's really easy for someone to tell you not to run from a problem when they're not facing it. They tell you to trust God and have faith, but they have no sympathy for your situation because they are simply regurgitating rhetoric. The truth is David needed to run. He trusted God completely, but that didn't mean that he was going to sit there while Saul attempted to take his life. When the spear is being hurled at you, it's ok to run, as long as you don't lose your faith in what God has promised you. God may even lead you right back to the king's chambers for another spear to be thrown, but that just means that you still have a little more dodging to do. God had no intentions of letting David be killed. Every spear that was thrown was on the exact flight path God intended. Every reflex of David was perfectly designed by the creator to make sure he could move as he needed to. Could God have miraculously stopped the spear? Or just killed Saul? Sure, but David would play a critical role in God's plan and he wasn't ready to be the man that God wanted him to be, so he had to run.

~

David's running lasted for years. And it wasn't just

running, it was running for his life. Saul wasn't content with David just running away, Saul hunted David. Saul wanted David dead. So, David lived the life of an outlaw. He was hunted and chased, day after day. There were good days when the sun was warm, and the enemies were far behind him. He could steal a little food from a field or rest underneath a shade tree, recovering just a little strength, but never forgetting that he was being pursued. But some days weren't this good. Some days he narrowly escaped the hunters. Some days he hid in the cold rain, waiting for the baying of the hounds to fade enough for him to seek some form of shelter. Such was the life of God's anointed.

Eventually, others who had had to make an escape from some sort of trouble or another began to find him. After a while, David assembled a small company of men. They worked together, helped each other, and watched out for each other, but they were still enemies of the state. They still spent their nights sleeping on cold, wet, cave floors. They were still hunted criminals. After this group grew in number, an extraordinary event took place. King Saul drew near, so close that David and his companions watched from the entrance of their cave, but Saul had no idea how close he was to his quarry.

1 Samuel 24 says that Saul ventured into the cave where David and his men were to attend to a personal need and while he was relieving himself, David's men saw an amazing opportunity. They told David that this was the time to free them - That this was what God

meant when He told David that He would deliver David's enemies into his hands. David could now end the running. David and his men could be free, and David could become king![66] Imagine how David felt as he quietly crossed the cave. This was the moment that would end his suffering and stop his life as a fugitive. This was the moment that could take him from sleeping on cave floors to sleeping in the palace. This must be God's opportunity. Or was it? I wonder what was going through David's mind as he crept up behind Saul. I like to think that something reminded David of Samuel pouring the oil on his head. His mind flashed back to that day in his father's house, with the prophet standing before him, anointing him in the presence of his family and in the presence of God Almighty. I believe it was at this moment when the Holy Spirit that came upon him powerfully that day in Bethlehem[68] whispered "This isn't the way it's supposed to happen."

And David listened.

Rather than kill Saul, David sneaks up behind him and cuts a small piece of his robe off and Saul has no clue anything happened[67]. Once Saul leaves, I can only imagine that David's men are furious. David wasn't the only one sleeping on the cave floors and living the life of a criminal. This wasn't just David's chance to return to society, it was theirs too. These men had been loyal to David and knew that they would be taken care of once David was king. David had just let their redemption walk away, losing nothing but a small piece of material from his robe. As David stood in the cave, holding the fabric in his hand, Imagine the conversation between David and his men.

"What have you done!?"

"You could have freed us!"

"Why did you spare His life!?"

"Why did you show your enemy mercy, knowing he would show you none!?"

"What loyalty do you owe him? He is no longer a godly king!"

David must have been torn inside at this point. This scene must have been strange for David and his men. They were also not accustomed to seeing their leader, the anointed future king of Israel, so broken. But at that moment, something happened inside David. That same Holy Spirit that so softly whispered to him that it was not time to end Saul's reign now grew from a whisper to a roar. Imagine David spinning to face his men, with a fire in his eye and a previously unheard ferocity in his voice and saying, "The Lord forbid that I should do such a thing to my master, the Lord's anointed, or lay my hand on him; for he is the anointed of the Lord.[69]" With this one sentence, David established God's order in his life and the lives of his men. He proclaimed, to both God and man, that he, David, would honor God above all else. David made it clear that the anointing of God was to be honored and held sacred. No matter how evil the king, he was still

God's anointed, and as such, was to be dealt with by God. David walked out of the cave and yelled to Saul, "My Lord, My King!"...and he bowed[70]

David's life after he was anointed exemplified perseverance, endurance, growth, fear, and patience. We often wonder why we are facing certain trials and certain things in our lives, but usually the answer is quite simple...God is helping you grow. Growth is very rarely fun, but it's necessary for us to accomplish the tasks that God lays before us. David reached a place where the anointing became real to him. He recognized that Saul was God's anointed and that only God was worthy of determining what happened to Saul. Even though Saul was rejected as king by God, God's anointing still rested on him because God still wanted Saul to serve a purpose in His plan. He wanted Saul to teach David about the anointing. He wanted to use Saul to teach David how to reach that place of broken humility in order to understand the moment he was anointed all those years ago. He wanted David to understand that because He had chosen David and anointed him as the future King of Israel, that nothing short of God Himself could remove David from his throne. He wanted David to understand that God had a plan, and David was a huge part of it. David and his men returned to the cave to spend the night. No warm beds, no freedom, no hot meal...only a cold, wet, cave floor. Most likely, the men still grumbled about their leader, but even then, there developed a newfound respect for David. Not for the man that lay beside them on the cave floor, but for the spirit of the one true God that radiated from the broken and desperate man.

David and his men learned that night that God's plan will oftentimes require a cave floor instead of a palace, because the cave floor is where we truly learn how wonderful it is to be called His Anointed.

~

Chapter 12
Bloodlines

~

Why was David so critical to God's plan of salvation?
To truly understand why David had to go through all
that he did, we have to jump back to Genesis, and take
a look at a few different people. The first person we'll
look into is Leah. Leah was the daughter of Laban,
sister of Rachel, and wife of Jacob. When Jacob visited
Laban and met Rachel, he loved Rachel and wanted to
marry her. He arranged to work for seven years for
Laban in return for Rachel's hand in marriage, but
when the time came to be married, Laban gave him
Leah instead. He said that it wasn't customary for the
younger daughter to marry first so Jacob would have to
work another seven years in order to be able to marry
Rachel[71].

Right off the bat, Leah must have felt pretty bad in this
relationship. Her father Laban's deception and trickery
were the only reasons she even had the opportunity to
be married in the first place. Jacob begrudgingly
accepted her as his wife and went to work to gain the
hand of the woman he actually loved, but God stepped
in to help Leah out. God saw that Jacob didn't love
Leah and that Leah was upset so he allowed her to
have children while Rachel couldn't[72]. This didn't seem
to help Leah much. Leah's first three children were
Reuben, Simeon, and Levi. When Reuben was born,
Leah said "It is because the Lord has seen my misery.

Surely my husband will love me now"[73]. After Simeon was born, she said, "Because the Lord heard that I am not loved, he gave me this one too."[74] After her third son, Levi, was born, Leah said, "Now at last my husband will become attached to me, because I have borne him three sons."[75] Three children, three very similar responses. Leah was so worried about being unloved, she refused to see the gifts that God was giving her. Her children were gifts from the Lord, babies that would grow into leaders of Israel. God would choose Levi's descendants to minister directly to him, but Leah couldn't see beyond her own poor circumstances God's blessing. After the birth of Levi, Leah became pregnant again and gave birth to a fourth son. This son she named Judah. The name Judah is derived from the Hebrew word for praise, and after his birth, Leah says "This time I will praise the Lord."[76] Leah finally took a step back from her troubles to reflect on what God was doing for her and offered up praise.

~

This leads us to focus on the next person. Do you think it's Judah? Good job. Judah was an altogether mixed-up guy. Judah was focused on in the book of Genesis more than any of his other brothers with the exception of Joseph, and most of the focus was bad. Judah wasn't a good guy. It was Judah who suggested that the brothers sell Joseph into slavery for profit. While he technically did keep his brothers from killing Joseph, it wasn't out of love, it was out of greed.[77] After Judah lead his brothers in selling Joseph, he had a particularly nasty run in with his daughter-in-law, thinking he was visiting a prostitute[78]. It was at this point that we kind of see him hit rock bottom, but a few chapters later we start to see something shift in Judah's line of thinking.

After being sold into slavery by his brothers, God blessed Joseph in such an incredible way that he became the second in command of all Egypt. While Joseph was in charge, a giant famine came across the land, but thanks to Joseph's planning, Egypt stored plenty of food. People from all over travelled to Egypt. Judah and the rest of Joseph's brothers, except Benjamin, showed up to buy food and Joseph was shocked. He recognized them, but they didn't recognize him, and he immediately accused them of being spies. The brothers tried to tell him who they were, but Joseph continued his ruse. Joseph finally tells them that one of the brothers must remain in prison in Egypt until the other brothers return with Benjamin, Joseph's full blood brother. The brothers left, Simeon remained behind, and Joseph waited. When the brothers return and tell Jacob what happened and that Benjamin must return with them, he adamantly opposes. He says he has already lost one son and he's not going to lose another.

This is the part of the story when we start to see Judah's change. In an effort to convince Jacob to send Benjamin to Egypt with the rest of the brothers, Reuben, his oldest son, proclaims responsibility for Benjamin and if anything happens, Jacob could kill Rueben's two sons. Really?! What kind of a deal is this? If Jacob was worried about losing one son, why would he risk that son knowing that the payback of losing him would be to lose two grandsons too? Luckily, Judah intervenes and does the honorable thing. Judah tells Jacob ``Send the boy along with me and we will go at once, so that we and you and our children may live and not die. I myself will guarantee his safety; you can hold me personally responsible for him. If I do not bring him back to you and set him here before you, I will bear the blame before you all my life"[79]. Jacob agrees and sends Benjamin with Judah.

Once back in Egypt, Joseph invited the brothers to dine with him, giving Benjamin five times the portions the other brothers received[80]. The next day, the brothers prepared to leave for home, but Joseph had a silver cup hidden in Benjamin's bag. As the brothers were leaving, someone came and accused them of stealing. They searched through everyone's belongings, found the silver cup in Benjamin's bag, and brought all of the brothers back to Joseph. Joseph was establishing an elaborate trap, and while this was seemingly random, this was actually all a test that Joseph had prepared for his brothers. Joseph was setting Benjamin up as the "favorite" and as a "dreamer"(silver cups were used to see the future), which were the exact things that his brothers hated about him all those years ago. Joseph wanted to see if his brothers had changed or if they would hate Benjamin in the same way they hated him. When they returned to Joseph, Judah, again stepped in. Judah explained the whole family dynamic and Jacob's love for Benjamin, stating that it would kill his father if they returned without him. Judah then said "Now then, please let your servant remain here as my lord's slave in place of the boy…"[81]. Judah once again showed his honor by being willing to sacrifice himself for the wellbeing of Benjamin. Joseph was moved by Judah's selfless act and finally revealed who he was to his brothers and there was a wonderfully happy reunion. Joseph brought his entire family to Egypt and they lived peacefully together for the rest of Jacob's life.

Years later, as Jacob is dying, he is passing out the blessings to his sons. While all of the sons receive blessing, Judah's was extra special.

Judah, your brothers will praise you; your hand will be on the neck of your enemies; your father's sons will bow down to you. You are a lion's cub, Judah; you return from the prey, my son. Like a lion he crouches and lies down, like a lioness – who dares to rouse him? The scepter will not depart from Judah, nor the ruler's staff from between his feet, until he to whom it belongs shall come and the obedience of the nations shall be his. He will tether his donkey to a vine, his colt to the choicest branch; he will wash his garments in wine, his robes in the blood of grapes. His eyes will be darker than wine, his teeth whiter than milk[82].

Judah's willingness to be a sacrifice was a foretelling of his bloodline. Judah's descendants ultimately became the Kings of Israel and the scepter never passed from this royal bloodline. The king's role was to embrace the opportunities to protect his people, to sacrifice for them, and to make sure that they were taken care of. Judah, hardly a good or moral man for most of his life, was part of God's perfect plan. Judah couldn't stop God's plan even if he wanted to. God was going to make something of Judah and his descendants and what was coming would shake the foundations of all of eternities creation to its core. The lion was coming.

~

So, what does Judah have to do with David? Well, the easy answer is that Judah was David's great, great, great, great, great, great, great, great, great, grandfather, but there was a little more to it than that. When God began his rescue plan His covenants with Noah and Abraham outlined God's promises to them. God used these promises to redeem His people from sin. Now, generations after His covenant with Abraham, another covenant was about to be established. This new covenant would be with a king from the line of Judah that would establish a dynasty to produce the greatest king ever known. There was only one problem: the current king was from the tribe of Benjamin.

Saul, the anointed king and a descendant of Benjamin, sat on the throne, while David was in exile. Though Saul would eventually be killed in battle and David would return from exile and claim the throne, there was still a little problem. David's took Saul's daughter to be his wife, keeping Saul's bloodline intact. The bloodline of King Saul, and Benjamin, would be enough for one of his descendants to claim rights to the throne of Israel. God needed a pure bloodline from the tribe of Judah.

As we've seen several times thus far on our short journey, God doesn't make mistakes. What we see as a problem, God sees as the plan. He never sat down and said, "Oh wow, I totally forgot that Saul wasn't from Judah!" God doesn't do surprised. He's all knowing and all powerful, and his plans are perfect. So, what was the plan? Well, it involved someone worshipping (that was a hint that worship is important...in case you missed it).

During David's reign as king, he established himself mightily in Israel. He conquered the Jebusites and the Philistines and solicited the help of his allies to help build a new palace[83]. David, eager to bring the Ark of the Covenant into Jerusalem so that God's presence would inhabit the kingdom, goes to Balaah, where the ark is being kept and loads the ark onto a wagon headed for Jerusalem. As they are traveling, one of the oxen that is pulling the cart trips and the ark shifts. Naturally not wanting the ark to tip off of the cart, one of the men helping, Uzzah, reaches out and touches the ark, and immediately dies[84]. David is horrified and is actually afraid of God at this moment. The Bible actually says that David asks, "How can the ark of the Lord ever come to me?"[85] David, in a moment of fear and doubt, determines that he is not worthy to be in the presence of God and sends it away to another place. For three months, the ark resides in the home of Obed-Edom, and God blesses this man and everything in his household. David is delaying his rightful blessings out of fear. He is the chosen and anointed King of Israel, God's anointed, but he is too afraid of his own potential failures to allow God to bless him. After a few months, David hears that God has blessed Obed-Edom and his home and comes to his senses. He retrieves the ark and brings it back to Jerusalem, and he brings it back in style. The level of celebration as David is bringing the ark from Obed-Edom to Jerusalem is hard to even imagine. David and his people bring the ark into Jerusalem with rejoicing. This is a party that has probably not happened in Jerusalem in a long time, if ever. Every time the people carrying the ark took 6 steps, David sacrificed a bull and a fattened calf[86]. That is a lot of cattle. I actually just did this experiment in my house. It would take me 3 bulls and 3 fattened calves to make it from my front door to my back door. The average person has a step distance of about 2 feet, there are 5,280 feet in a mile, which means that one mile will average about 2600 steps. One mile would require David to sacrifice about 440 bulls and 440 calves. That is a seriously large sacrifice. As David follows the ark into the city, sacrificing to the Lord and rejoicing, he's also dancing. David, wearing a linen ephod, danced before the Lord "with all of his might"[87]. David wasn't just tapping his foot, David was dancing. David praised God because God's presence was coming into his city. David worshipped because he remembered the anointing all of those years ago back in Bethlehem and his God, the God that chose him, the God that created everything, was entering into his city...and he was excited.

We lose sight of the importance of worship in our lives today both in corporate worship in our churches as well as the worship that exists in our own lives personally. We were created to worship because we were created by a God that is worthy to be worshipped. We come together on Sunday mornings and we sing 3 songs that make us smile or get a little excited because the back beat is really intense. There might be a piano piece that just gives you goosebumps or maybe a lyric about what God has done for us even makes us shed a tear. We've turned worship into an emotion, and that is exactly what our enemy wants to happen. We feel the tingle of the music and mistake it for the Holy Spirit, and do you know why? We make this mistake because our enemy is brilliant. Do you think that our enemy doesn't know music theory in a way that we can't understand? Do you not think that he knows exactly how each musical note can subconsciously affect our psyche? Performers have used tricks with music and color to affect their audiences for years. Next time you are at a live play or concert, pay attention to the music and colors of the lights during the scenes and songs. Notice how the lights begin to migrate closer to pink when the subject is love and compassion. You begin to see blues during the peaceful and tranquil moments and yellows during the joyful happy times. The music follows the colors or vice versa. This is not done by accident. The set designers are trying to draw out your emotion because your emotion is what stimulates a response. It's also no accident that our minds work this way. God's design for us is amazing. Modern day science is baffled by the way we're wired. There are things going on in our brains we don't even know about yet because of how complex God made us. But our enemy knows some of those complexities too, and he knows how to exploit them. He knows that presenting obvious evil won't work. While the sound of us singing "Holy, Holy, Holy" makes him cringe, he knows that an emotional reaction will often make us feel content. He's relying on being able to draw our focus back to whatever it is that he has in front of us as soon as that song is over, distracting us from what God really wants...relationship. Worship isn't about emotion, it's not about tears, it's not about goosebumps. Yes, all of those might show up when we worship, but worship is about God. Worship is about assigning God His rightful place in our lives. It's about humbling ourselves before our all-powerful creator and telling Him that He is in control. It's about laying down every single thing in our lives before His throne and saying, "All I have is me, but I'm yours." Emotion can't defeat evil. Emotion can't claim victory over circumstances. Emotion can't stop the armies of hell from moving into our homes or our churches, and emotion certainly can't keep us in the presence of God. But when our relationship with our creator is real, and we enter into a place of worship that is personal between us and our wonderful God, that will stop every single advance the enemy comes to attempt.

I feel like before we continue, I should throw a disclaimer out and ask you not to chase down your worship leader next Sunday and ask him why he's toying with your emotions. It's ok to have lighting effects and great music. God gave us tools to minister His glory and it's ok to use them. In fact, if your focus during worship is on the lights and music and not on worshipping our King, please go back and read the previous paragraph again. I'm not trying to be mean, but before we complain about the performance side of our corporate worship, we need to make 100% sure that we're not focusing on the performance instead of worshipping. Focusing on something with good intentions is still focusing on it.

Now, back to King David. David was dancing and worshipping God. The king was in the streets, in the midst of the servants, acting very "unkingly". Kings maintained a sense of regalness and refinement and were to be looked upon with admiration. And here was David, dancing and rejoicing in front of everyone, and it didn't set well with his wife. David's wife, Michal, was Saul's daughter, and a descendant of the tribe of Benjamin. Michal loved David, but Michal, much like her father, did not love the Lord. She played the part as needed, but there was no relationship. As David came into the palace after the ark was brought into the city, Michal approached him and said, "How the king of Israel has distinguished himself today, going around half-naked in full view of the slave girls of his servants as any vulgar fellow would!"[88] Now, David wasn't running around in the nude here, but he was wearing an ephod, which was the top part of a garment the priests wore. This was sleeveless and came down to probably mid-thigh, but it fell far short of the kingly robes that Michal expected her husband to be wearing. What Michael was really saying was "What are you doing acting like a commoner? You're embarrassing yourself, and me, in front of the servants." David's reply is one of the greatest responses in all of the Bible. 2nd Samuel 6:21-22 say:

"It was before the Lord, who chose me rather than your father or anyone from his house when he appointed me ruler over

the Lord's people Israel — I will celebrate before the Lord. I will become even more undignified than this, and I will be humiliated in my own eyes. But by these slave girls you spoke of, I will be held in honor."

Do you see it? "I will become EVEN MORE undignified than this, and I WILL BE HUMILIATED IN MY OWN EYES...". David didn't care what anyone thought because He was worshipping. He didn't care what his wife thought, he didn't care what the servants thought, he didn't care what the priests thought, he only cared about what God thought. He was so focused on his relationship with God that he blocked everything else out and just danced before God.

Dancing before God was what allowed David to be "undignified before the Lord", but your action may be something completely different. We each have a different level of "humiliation" that we must reach before God. God doesn't want us to be embarrassed, and I assure you that the drive of the Holy Spirit is not to make you do something that will cause you grief, but many times what we view as humiliation in our eyes is simply doing something a little outside of our comfort zone. "Becoming undignified before the Lord" to you might be lifting a hand in worship, singing or praying out loud, or telling someone at the gas station that Jesus loves them and why. The truth is, I can't tell you what God might be pushing you towards. I can tell you that the more you worship, the more you begin to feel the constraints of others drop off of you and your relationship with God becomes so much more intense. Michal couldn't see this, and she was angry and jealous. She was mad that David cared more about God than about the royal image, and God used this situation to break Saul's bloodline forever. 2nd Samuel 6:23 says:

> *And Michal daughter of Saul had no children to the day of her death.*

Just like that, the bloodline of Judah, the bloodline of David, was purified. The future kings of Israel would descend from the tribe of Judah and Saul's bloodline was no longer in the picture. God's plans are always perfect and there is never a time that He's not completely in control. While we tend to focus on the problems, God is focused on us. He continually reminds us that He has every problem that we're facing already figured out, so quit worrying and worship. When the trials present themselves, worship. When hard times show up, find that place where you can spend time in the presence of the King of Kings. You have no ability to break the bloodlines of your past. There is nothing that you can do to get rid of Saul's blood in your life other than worship. God has already redeemed and anointed you to be His child, His creation, His beloved.

~

Part 4

Patient Love

~

He stood on the bank of the river, the great kingdom of Babylon stretched out before him on the opposite side, watching her. She was there, beneath a willow, weeping, and her tears brought both heartache and joy to Him. Heartache that He had to see her in this state, yet joy knowing that she indeed remembered Him and was ready to come home. It had been so long since she had smiled at Him, sought him, desired to be near Him, but each time He thought of her, He smiled. Each time she walked away, He pursued her, and His desire burned more and more intense for her each day. He loved her more than anything, and there was nothing that she would ever do to make that stop. As he stood watching His Beloved, her head slowly turned upward, and her eyes locked on Him. From across the river, He could see the tears of her bondage glistening on her cheeks, but then, a smile as she recognized Him. Their eyes held each other's gaze for what seemed an eternity, until a beautiful song of praise broke forth from her lips, and now it was His turn to weep. Through His tears, He knew that it was almost complete. The final part of the plan was in motion, and soon, nothing would ever keep Him from His Beloved.

~

Chapter 13
A Perfect Promise

~

So where do we go from here you may be wondering? We've journeyed from creation to David. We've looked at a lot of different people in the story, and quite honestly, it's a lot to grasp. Trying to walk through history from Abraham to David and connect the dots of God's salvation plan is a big task, and we're only hitting the high points. At this point in our journey, David is the established and anointed king of Israel, the first king of the tribe of Judah, and the first of the dynasty that will ultimately produce the Messiah. These are facts that we're already familiar with, so I suppose we could just jump over the rest of the Old Testament and get right to Christ. We know that Christ was born of the tribe of Judah, and now we know how the tribe of Judah came to rule Israel, so what more is there to really cover? I mean, Christ is the savior. He's the seed that God planted all those years ago. He is the one that changed everything and allowed us back into communion with God, so why not just skip everything else and get straight to Him? I'll tell you why. It's because the promise of Christ and the events leading up to his coming are a huge part of how we are able to see how much God truly loves us. Apart from Christ actually stretching His arms out on the cross and dying for us, there is no greater example of God's love for us than His relationship with Israel. If we were to only look at the gift of grace, but not the past events that led us to need the grace, can we truly appreciate the grace given? The fact that Christ was willing to sacrifice Himself for us, a people so wretched and unworthy, is an amazing demonstration of love on its own. When we add in the events leading up to sacrifice, we begin to see how extraordinary that love really is.

So then, let's stick around in the Old Testament just a little bit longer, shall we? Second Samuel chapters six and seven are pivotal chapters in God's redemption plan for mankind in so many ways. Not only do these chapters show how big God is, that He can break and establish bloodlines and kingdoms at will, but they show how important true worship to the King of Kings is. If we recall the requirements that God laid out for the King of Israel in Deuteronomy, one of them was that he would be righteous. The establishment of a righteous king was the way God was going to save His people. William J Dumbrell wrote, in regard to 2 Samuel chapters 6 and 7:

What is thus being said by the sequence of these chapters, is that Yahweh's kingship must be first provided for before the question of Israel's can be taken up. Only when such an acknowledgement of Yahweh's rule has been made may the possibility of a firmly established Israelite royal line be discussed.[89]

What he is saying here is that God's kingdom needed to be glorified first, not Israel's. David experienced plenty of things in his life thus far that offered cause for celebration, but the fact that he humbled himself in worship showed God that he was indeed the right person to reign over Israel. Now, of course, God already knew this, but with mankind, there is always the element of freewill. God knows what's going to happen, but He will always allow us to make the decision to worship or not worship for ourselves.

David's willingness to humble himself before God leads to the greatest promise that David ever received. In 2 Samuel 7, we find David talking with the prophet Nathan. David worries that he is not giving God His glory because he is living in a palace, while the Ark of the Covenant is residing in a tent[90]. I don't know about you, but I've always found this part of the story just a little bit comical. Here is David, the mighty king, chosen and anointed by God, a man after God's own heart, feeling like he needs to show God some respect and build Him a house. David wants God to have a palace that shows off His magnificence and is feeling bad that he's living in a house better than God. It's a noble sentiment to be sure, but one that was a bit misguided. Later that night, God tells Nathan that David's plan isn't God's plan and has him go and deliver a message to David.

What God instructs Nathan to tell David is outlined in 2 Samuel 7:5-17, and I love the way God starts out. Right or wrong, I always seem to picture God with a little bit of an exasperated look on his face when He's talking to us. I know that He most likely isn't looking at us with an astonished and dumbfounded look on his face, wondering what in the world is going through our heads, but when I read His responses to His children sometimes, I can see how a dumbfounded look might be justified. Remember, David is talking about building a big house for God. He's feeling bad that he's living in a palace and God is in a tent, and God basically says, "I don't need a house, I'm capable of handling that part of things, you just listen to this next part." While David's intentions were pure, he overlooked the fact that God was bigger than the Ark of the Covenant. God is bigger than a tent. God is bigger than a royal palace. God didn't need a house but if He wanted a house, He could easily make that happen without David's charity. Now, please don't take what I'm saying and dismiss all of the wonderful things that we can do with a nice church. I'm not saying that we need to quit making our buildings nice or anything like that. I'm simply pointing out that when we determine that our buildings and image are what defines how big our God is, we're dreadfully close to seeing God leave that building, if He hasn't already.

God isn't mad at David, though. He's actually quite pleased. David, while a bit presumptuous in his ambitions to build God a great house, genuinely desired to see God glorified. He wanted to see God placed above everything else, including himself, and that is exactly why God told David the next part. God gave David, through Nathan, an amazing promise that solidified the path to our wonderful salvation and God's ultimate plan of redemption.

There are two major parts of this promise that God gives David, with the first being captured in 2 Samuel 7:8-11 (NIV):

Now then, tell my servant David, 'This is what the Lord Almighty says: I took you from the pasture, from tending the flock, and appointed you ruler over my people Israel. I have been with you wherever you have gone, and I have cut off all your enemies from before you. Now I will make your name great, like the names of the greatest men on earth. And I will provide a place for my people Israel and will plant them so that they can have a home of their own and no longer be disturbed. Wicked people will not oppress them anymore, as they did at the beginning and have done ever since the time I appointed leaders over my people Israel. I will also give you rest from all your enemies.

God is reassuring David that he is chosen. He wants David to know beyond the shadow of any doubt that God is with him forever. He tells David that he would become a great king, and that he would be remembered forever. He also reaffirms the promises He made to Abraham all those years ago. He tells David that Israel would have a place of their own where they would no longer be oppressed. This promise alone was probably making David get pretty excited, but just wait until you see the next part. Second Samuel 7:11-16 (NIV) says:

"The Lord declares to you that the Lord himself will establish a house for you: When your days are over and you rest with your ancestors, I will raise up your offspring to succeed you, your own flesh and blood, and I will establish his kingdom. He is the one who will build a house for my Name, and I will establish the throne of his kingdom forever. I will be his father, and he will be my son. When he does wrong, I will punish him with a rod wielded by men, with floggings inflicted by human hands. But my love will never be taken away from him, as I took it away from Saul, whom I removed

from before you. Your house and your kingdom will endure forever before me; your throne will be established forever.'"

Have you noticed that when God makes a promise, He really makes a promise? There are no weak promises from God. God's not telling David that the next few years would work out, God is telling David that He is going to establish an eternal dynasty, starting with him.

There are four very important things about this promise that we need to hone in on in order to really grasp the magnitude of it. The first is that this promise is unconditional. Just like the promises that God made to Noah, Abraham, Jacob, and Moses, nothing was required from David for this promise to be fulfilled. This was God making a promise, no works needed, just ears to hear it.

The next three things we need to see are based on the wording of God's promise. God specifically promises David three things in verse 16: his house, his kingdom, and his throne, will all be established forever. This is so incredibly important because this is the promise of the Messiah! This is how Christ would soon arrive on the scene! God established the bloodline! The earlier part of this promise referred to David's son Solomon, who would actually build the temple, or house, for God that David wanted to build, but the next part takes away the immediate future and focuses on eternity. God was formally establishing David's bloodline as the royal bloodline for all of eternity. Christ, descended from the 'house' of David, would reign over David's 'kingdom', from David's 'throne' forever. Not only did this fulfill the requirements of the king that God set forth in Deuteronomy, but it solidified that path to eternal salvation for God's creation that He so dearly loved.

The Davidic Covenant changed the course of history for Israel and for everyone in the future. God had honored his promises to Abraham of making a great nation of his descendants. He had brought them into the land that He had told Abraham would be theirs. Now, God was formally beginning stage two of his plan. This promise to David set the stage for the greatest sacrifice and act of love mankind, and all of eternity, would ever know. And while this promise would be tested over the next several generations, this perfect promise, to the king that was once a simple shepherd, began the march towards the restoration of God's beloved.

~

Chapter 14
Love in Anger

~

I'm going to come right out and tell you guys
something...I'm a huge fan of the Old Testament.
While so many people who claim a knowledge of God's
love today never stray from the gospels and epistles of
the New Testament, I tend to spend most of my time in
the Old. Now, I fully believe that there is never a bad
part of the Bible to read and if you find Romans to be
super powerful and it speaks to you every time you
read it, then by all means, dive into Romans as deep as
you can. I feel this way about the books of Exodus and
Joshua. I love to read them, and when I am struggling,
those are the places I usually turn. However, we have
to remember that the Bible is the inspired word of
God...all of it. We can't stay in one part or the other, we
have to read all of it. If we focus on the Old Testament
without the New Testament, we can never see what
God was doing through all of the people before Christ.
We would never be able to wrap our minds around his
wonderful love for us, because we would never know
about Christ himself and the sacrifice that He made.
Likewise, if we spend all of our time in the New
Testament, we miss out on how long God's love waited
for us. We miss out on how perfectly designed His
plan for us to become reunited with Him really was.
While some parts of the Bible may seem a little hard to
wrap our minds around, it becomes a little easier when
we start to look at them with the entire timeline of

creation to Christ in our field of view.

One of the sections of the Bible that I think intimidates many people is the prophetic books. The major and minor prophets that make up the last 17 books of the Old Testament can be a little difficult to digest. When we read these books, we typically cringe a bit at how mean and angry God is, but this is where our knowledge of what He has already done for his people, combined with our knowledge of what Christ is going to do, sheds a whole new light on things. It's also helpful to understand the time frame when these books were written, because it's this time that Israel was really testing God's love and the prophets were playing a major role in God's plan. The general consensus among most scholars is that the prophetic books were written between about 850BC to 450BC and cover a period of time of around 200 or so years prior to the exile of Israel and Judah, through their exile, and about 100 years or so after their return. It's this period of time that we begin to see God's warnings to His people increase through the prophets. We see God's anger growing and his patience running thin with His chosen nation because of the terrible things they are doing and their dismissal of Him as their one true Lord.

So, if God's getting angry and warning the Israelites of disaster, how are these books about love? Well, in truth, all 66 books of the Bible are about love...we read some parts of them and see the anger, but in the anger, there is great love. We've discussed already that God's love is real and powerful, even in his anger, and this is no exception. One of the best examples of this love is found in the book of Jeremiah. Jeremiah 17:9-10 says:

> *The heart is deceitful above all things, and*
> *desperately sick; who can understand it? I the Lord*
> *search the heart and test the mind.*

Doesn't really scream "I love you", does it? When
we read it without the context of God's plan of
salvation, no, it's kind of off putting. But think
about what God is saying here through Jeremiah.
It helps to think about Paul's words in Romans
when he says, "I do not understand the things I do,
for what I want to do I do not do, but what I hate I
do."[91] Jeremiah and Paul are saying very similar
things. We can feel the evil that is in our own
hearts and the sickness that evil causes. We know
right from wrong, and even though we recognize
it, we still fall into sin every day...but God searches
our heart and knows us. He knows us better than
we know ourselves and He wants to help us not
give in to the sickness in our hearts. How?
Through relationship. He's right there with us, all
the time, never leaving, searching our hearts and
calling out to us to come into His great love.

Another great example is found in the book of
Jonah. We all know the story of Jonah being sent
to Nineveh to warn the Ninevites of God's coming
judgement. The Ninevites were wicked people and
God had decided that He had enough and sent
Jonah with a final warning...repent or be
destroyed. Doesn't really sound loving does it?
God didn't' want to destroy Nineveh, but He also
wouldn't let them breed evil that would further

infiltrate His chosen people. God's mercy and love though is so amazing that He gave them one more shot. Jonah 3:8-10 says:

"Let everyone turn from his evil way and from the violence that is in his hands. Who knows? God may turn and relent and turn from his fierce anger, so that we may not perish." When God saw what they did, how they turned from their evil way, God relented of the disaster that he had said he would do to them, and he did not do it.

God offered Nineveh a chance to repent, and when they did, He forgave them. Without possessing amazing love for His creation, He would not have been able to extend this mercy. Although the Ninevites eventually turned from God again, He was still willing to afford them forgiveness if they would just come back to Him.

While the story of Jonah and the Ninevites is an amazing example of God's love and mercy, there is perhaps no greater illustration in the Old Testament than the book of Hosea. Hosea lived as a prophet in Israel right before they were conquered by the Assyrian's and sent into exile. In the first chapter of Hosea, verse 2, God tells Hosea

Go, marry a promiscuous woman and have children with her, for like an adulterous wife this land is guilty of unfaithfulness to the Lord.

I can't really imagine how Hosea must have felt when he received this command, I imagine he was probably a little upset, but he remained faithful and married a woman named Gomer. Next, God told Hosea to have children and had him name them some terrible things, and then he was to instruct the children to run their mother off because she had been unfaithful. Chapter two of the book of Hosea parallels Hosea and Gomer's relationship with that of God and Israel and is a clear example of how God has viewed Israel as an adulterous wife and has to send her away...but then there is chapter 3. In Hosea chapter 3, God tells Hosea to go and find his unfaithful wife and love her, just like God loved Israel. He was to bring her back into his home and make her his faithful wife, and vow to be faithful to her also, just like God would do with Israel.

Hosea must have had a pretty miserable section of life while all of this was going on, but it was nothing compared to the heartbreak that God experienced watching His chosen people turn their backs on Him and walk away. The illustration of Hosea and Gomer is a human representation of God's love for Israel. God knew that His people would be unfaithful, but He still created them, provided for them, loved them, delivered them, and established them as a nation, set apart. He knew that they would sin and that the only way to protect them from their sin was to send them away for a time. It was while the Israelites were in exile that they refocused their attention on God and remembered who he was. Hosea 3:4-5 says:

For the Israelites will live many days without king or prince, without sacrifice or sacred stones, without ephod or household gods. Afterward the Israelites will return and seek the Lord their God and David their king. They will come trembling to the Lord and to his blessings in the last days.

This punishment would ultimately prepare the way for God to begin the final stages of his masterful plan to restore His beloved creation. Through His righteous anger, His perfect love was put on display for us. It's easy to read books like Jeremiah, Jonah, and Hosea and wonder how we can refer to God in the Old Testament as a god of mercy. But when we look at the entire plan, knowing what was coming from the line of kings that God established through David, we see His amazing plan working out. There is a special passage of scripture that I hold onto in my life that always reminds me of how great God is, and this reminder was given to the Israelites during this time period. Isaiah 43:1-3:

But now thus says the Lord, he who created you, O Jacob, he who formed you, O Israel: "Fear not, for I have redeemed you; I have called you by name, you are mine. When you pass through the waters, I will be with you; and through the rivers, they shall not overwhelm you; when you walk through fire you shall not be burned, and the flame shall not consume you. For I am the Lord your God, the Holy One of Israel, your Savior."

He has called me by name! He has called you by name! When we pass through the waters, He will be with us! The rivers will not overwhelm us! The fire will not burn or consume us! Because He is our God, and He is HOLY! God is a god of love and mercy and He had this love and mercy on display for His people throughout their darkest times. In the midst of idolatry, debauchery, and a myriad of other sins, He never stopped loving His chosen people. Though He got angry and allowed them to be ta ken away for a brief time, for their own protection, He never abandoned them. He never forsook them. He never gave up on his plan to redeem His Beloved.

Chapter 15
The Promise Revealed

Have you ever heard of The Forbidden Chapter in the Bible? It's pretty cool to think about, right? Honestly, when I think about something called The Forbidden Chapter I immediately think of some type of fantasy, Lord of the Rings-type story where they have to interpret the sacred text of an ancient writing to see some great treasure. It's pretty amazing to think about, but what's even more amazing is that describes Isaiah 53 perfectly. Sure, there are no elves, orcs, dwarfs, or any other Tolkien characters, but there is a promise, written some 600 years or so before Christ that told of the coming savior...of the Messiah.

So why is it forbidden? Well, it's technically not forbidden but it has been ignored in many circles for many years now and has been given the nickname The Forbidden Chapter by some. The reason it has been ignored is because it was a promise, made to a group of people that God loved, that was missed. This promise to God's chosen nation, that He would send them a savior that would rescue and restore them, was ignored and abused. The promise of a Messiah was lost by the very people to whom it was made.

Where would we be without this one chapter? I'm not talking about missing out on the countless different Easter videos discussing the crucifixion and resurrection of Christ...I'm talking about eternity. True, this single prophecy from Isaiah wasn't itself a requirement for Christ's arrival. No, it's the message that Isaiah relayed that makes such a huge difference in our lives. The message that God loves us so much that He was willing to offer this type of gift to a people who so blatantly turned their back on Him that makes us pay so much attention to this chapter. He promised a savior, even though we don't deserve one.

As I have spent the last several weeks trying to figure out how to write this chapter, how to best describe the words written so many years ago by Isaiah, the words spoken by our loving God, I have come up blank time and time again. How do you break down a prophecy so specific to what our savior was going to do for us and analyze it? How do you choose which parts to focus on and which not to mention? Each time I would begin, thinking I had my mind wrapped around how I wanted to dive into God's love for us with a verse or two from Isaiah 53, something else would jump out at me. Each time I read it, I was more and more amazed at how I could feel both joyous and heartbroken at the same time. I felt ecstatic that God loves me this much and yet sorrowful that each day I heap these same portions on Him through my sinful nature, and even more so for those that are missing it all together.

When I think of Christ's interactions with the Pharisees and other religious leaders, I'm amazed at how they so irreverently dismissed him as the

Messiah because they weren't even trying to look for a savior. They knew what Isaiah 53 other prophecies said about recognizing Christ, but they didn't want to see Him. They wanted to continue their earthly roles, living good lives and elevating themselves above others. They didn't see because they didn't want to see. Fast forward to today and churches are filled every week with men and women who refuse to acknowledge and accept what Christ has done for them. The "Christian" religion is one of the largest in the world, yet what percentage of "Christians" are truly able to read through Isaiah 53 and recognize that it was their transgressions that Christ was pierced for. How many of you can honestly say right now that the fact Christ was crushed for your iniquities actually means something to you? Do you realize that your life was purchased by the man outlined in Isaiah 53, and more importantly, do you not recognize the price? He was perfect, knew no sin, knew no guilt, yet was assigned a grave with the wicked. He took every ounce of sin and shame from us. He took the unthinkable punishment - not death, but true separation from God - so that we didn't have to.

As I sit here writing, I wonder how best to emphasize what Isaiah 53 is saying, and Hebrews 4:12 begins to ring out in my mind:

For the word of God is alive and active. Sharper than any double-edged sword, it penetrates even to dividing soul and spirit, joints and marrow; it judges the thoughts and attitudes of the heart.

What better way for us all to really understand God's word than to read it. I know it's easy to skim-read things. You have breezed over the bulk of the scriptures I've referenced in this book thus far haven't you? You're not alone. We know most of these by heart, so we jump to the end and move on. I'm guilty of doing the same, and I honestly almost copied and pasted this passage directly into this page, but I didn't. I typed every word, because I refuse to allow what my Jesus did for me to be skimmed through. Does my typing this scripture make me closer to Him? No, but it's not the action, it's the intent, and that's what reading, and asking God to speak to you while reading, is all about. I implore you right now: If you read nothing else in this book beyond this chapter, I pray that you will read this following passage, and that you will see God's love for you in it. It is my prayer that the words of God through Isaiah spark something in you that had previously not been lit and that a newfound fire would be ignited because of the love of our Savior. I genuinely hope that these words remind you that this was the seed, the plan, that God had designed generations prior, to bring His Beloved, you, back to Him.

~

Who has believed our message, and to whom has the arm of the Lord been revealed? He grew up before him like a tender shoot, and like a root out of dry ground. He had no beauty or majesty to attract us to him, nothing in his appearance that we should desire him. He was despised and rejected by mankind, a man of suffering, and familiar with pain. Like one from whom people hid their faces he was despised, and we held him in low esteem. Surely he took up our pain and bore our suffering, yet we considered him punished by God, stricken by him, and afflicted. But he was pierced for our transgressions, he was crushed for our iniquities; the punishment that brought us peace was on him, and by his wounds we are healed. We all, like sheep, have gone astray, each of us has turned to our own way; and the Lord has laid on him the iniquity of us all. He was oppressed and afflicted, yet he did not open his mouth; he was led like a lamb to the slaughter, and as a sheep before its shearers is silent, so he did not open his mouth. By oppression and judgement he was taken away. Yet who of his generation protested? For he was cut off from the land of the living; for the transgression of my people he was punished. He was assigned a grave with the wicked, and with the rich in his death, though he had done no violence, nor was any deceit in his mouth. Yet it was the Lord's will to crush him and cause him to suffer, and though the Lord makes his life an offering for sin, he will see his offspring and prolong his days, and the will of the Lord will prosper in his hand. After he has suffered, he will see the light of life and be satisfied; by his knowledge my righteous servant will justify many, and he will bear their iniquities. Therefore I will give him a portion among the great and he will divide the spoils with the strong, because he poured out his life unto death, and was numbered with the transgressors. For he bore the sin of many and made intercession for the transgressors.

Isaiah 53

~

Chapter 16
The Past Reflected

~

As I scan over the last two chapters, I can't help but laugh just a little and think that was probably one of the most high-level overviews of the prophetic books of the Bible one could possibly give. I highly suggest spending some time in the prophetic books if you have not but do so with this one thing in mind. Don't try to understand every word, ask God to reveal what He intends for you at that moment. I think one of the greatest mistakes we make when we read God's word is expecting some form of revelation to help us with whatever issue we are facing at that exact moment in time. God's word is just that, His word...how he speaks to us...and if we want relationship, we have to just be in His word. We have to spend time reading it, studying it, and loving it for no other reason than that this is what our wonderful God gave us. The more we enjoy the time we get to spend with God, the more He will reveal to us.

We have seen some pretty high-level stuff of how God spoke through the prophets to prepare people to see His promise of salvation come to fruition. Now we'll jump ahead and see how a few of them were actually fulfilled, specifically around the birth of Jesus Christ. The very first book of the New Testament introduces us to a phrase that always seems to get just a bit glossed over, but it's all over the place. Matthew wrote in Matthew 1:22:

All this took place to fulfill what the Lord had said through the prophet...

This phrase is a pretty simple statement that I'm sure you've noticed right? This particular verse is generally always referenced at Christmas, and to give most pastors credit, they point out the Old Testament prophecy to which Matthew is referring. But here is what's cool. Matthew used this phrase dozens of times in his writing. Matthew 2:15, 2:17, 2:23, 4:14, 8:17, and 12:17 are just a few of the many times Matthew referenced prophecies from the Old Testament to let his readers know that He wasn't making up this stuff. He was pointing to history, to written works from the same people that the religious leaders of the day quoted, to make sure that his account was validated.

Matthew was indeed a detail-oriented writer, which fit given that the first 16 verses of his book are genealogy. I'm sure that most of you are like me when it comes to genealogy and find it a bit boring. There are times when I have to really force myself to read through the beginnings of 1 Chronicles, but when I began studying our path from sin to salvation, something really cool jumped out at me that made me rethink genealogy. There were 14 generations from Abraham to David, 14 generations from David to when the Israelites went into exile in Babylon, and 14 generations from exile to Jesus Christ[92]. Why is this so cool? Do some quick math...14 is a multiple of 7, which is God's number of completion. Three sets of 14 is 42. 42!! Seriously?! Come on, no one else thinks that is cool?! Go on, ask Alexa "What's the meaning of life, the universe, and everything?" What did she say? Read *Hitchhiker's Guide to the Galaxy,* and what did the supercomputer come up with as the ultimate meaning of life?!?! FORTY!!!! TWO!!!! Ok, Ok, I'm obviously being super sarcastic here about the number 42, but don't you find it just the least bit awesome that Jesus Christ even influences pop culture without us realizing it a lot of times? There is a pretty cool bit of real significance in this though...42 is six sets of 7 (7x6=42). On the seventh day, God rested. Jesus Christ is the beginning of the seventh...Jesus Christ is our sabbath, our rest! That is a pretty cool thought to me. There is also a ton of really interesting reading in the book of Daniel, specifically chapter nine, around this math, but I'll leave that for the prophecy home groups to discuss.

Anyway, I got a little bit further into forty-two than I intended to, so let's get back to the book of Matthew and his genealogy. One of the really cool things that I picked up on as I began reading through Matthew's genealogy of Christ is how many prophecies are referenced as fulfilled in a simple genealogy. In the first six verses alone, Matthew points to the fulfilling of six Old Testament prophecies. Don't believe me? Check this out, the first six verses of Matthew chapter 1 as bullet points:

- Abraham (Genesis 12:3) the father of Isaac
- Isaac (Genesis 26:4) the father of Jacob

- Jacob (Genesis 28:14) the father of Judah and his brothers
- Judah (Genesis 49:8-10) the father of Perez and Zerah, whose mother was Tamar
- Perez the father of Hezron
- Hezron the father of Ram
- Ram the father of Amminadab
- Amminadab the father of Nahshon
- Nahshon the father of Salmon,
- Salmon the father of Boaz, whose mother was Rahab,
- Boaz the father of Obed, whose mother was Ruth,
- Obed the father of Jesse
- and Jesse (Isaiah 11) the father of King David (Isaiah 9:7-8)

For the sake of space, I won't delve into each one of those scriptures, but do check them out. We've talked already about God's promises to Abraham, Isaac, and Jacob, how God established Judah as the royal line in Israel, and the Davidic Covenant and God's promise to David to establish an eternally ruling dynasty from his bloodline. God's promises are not empty promises, and Christ is the fulfillment of those promises. Matthew, in a simple genealogy, put every question about Jesus Christ legitimacy as the heir of King David and as the prophesied Messiah to rest.

Matthew continues his confirmation of Christ's role as the Messiah after his genealogy by talking about his mother. In Matthew 1:23, Matthew says:

The virgin will conceive and give birth to a son, and they will call him Immanuel" (which means "God with us")

What Matthew is referencing is Isaiah 7:4:

Therefore the Lord himself will give you a sign: The virgin will conceive and give birth to a son, and will call him Immanuel.

In the following chapter, after Christ was born, Matthew continues his historical support of Christ as the Messiah. In Matthew 2, the Magi from the east had come and asked King Herod where the newborn king was. Matthew 2:4 says (speaking of Herod):

When he had called together all the people's chief priests and teachers of the law, he asked them where the Messiah was to be born.

The answer that Herod's people gave him was directly from Micah 5:2:

But you, Bethlehem Ephrathah, though you are small among the clans of Judah, out of you will come for me one who will be ruler over Israel, whose origins are from of old, from ancient times.

Once Herod determines where Christ was born, he sends out his horrible order to execute all of the male babies under the age of two[93], confirming the prophecy of Jeremiah, in Jeremiah 31:15:

A voice is heard in Ramah, mourning and great weeping, Rachel weeping for her children and refusing to be comforted, because they are no more

Matthew's account of the early years of Christ's life is just one small section of confirmations used by New Testament authors to confirm Christ as our Messiah. I suppose that one could argue there was no true need for Matthew or any of the others to document these things. God had already proven time and time again that His plan would unfold, unimpeded, but He also knew that there would be skeptics. God's love for us always, and forever, allows us to decide for ourselves whether or not to believe in Him. Freewill is one of the things that makes us so much greater than any of His other creations. While everything else worships Him because they are made to do so, we worship Him because we so choose. We were created to be in communion with Him, but we were given the choice also. It's this freewill that makes Matthew's and other New Testament writer's accounts of Christ so important. God could have skipped centuries of watching His beloved children walk away from Him. He's God, He can do that, but He didn't want to...He wanted us to see His incredible love for us and to run into His wonderful and loving arms of our own volition. New Testament writings that reference prophecies hundreds of years prior remind us how loving God really is. They remind us of His patient waiting for us and how perfect His plan is. My seven year old son told my wife a while back that the Old Testament was "a cycle of apostasy". I'm sure he heard this on one of his shows we watch, but it was so true...and a little funny. We look back at the Israelites in the Old Testament, God's chosen people, and we cringe at the number of times they turned their backs on God. The Old Testament, each and every book, is a perfect painting of the patient love that our God had and still has for us. We see Him forgive and rescue repeatedly, knowing full well that His people would just walk away again...but he continued to do it.

When we read historical accounts, it's always easy to see the flaws, but it's not easy to see the similar mistakes we are making in our lives today. We offer up excuses based on scripture for why we can't press into God. We're too tired to wake up and spend time in His word because we were serving at a local outreach until late the night before. We couldn't focus too much on our fellowship or the needs of others on Sunday morning because we were far too busy making sure that we had our area of ministry ready. We didn't stop and simply tell God thank you for all of His blessings because we needed to hurry up and drop a load of groceries off to someone who needed them. Please don't think that I'm criticizing our generosity, outreaches and churches. I use the three examples above because I can relate. James 2 tells us that faith and works must go hand in hand[94], so we can't stop ministering to those who need to hear about God's wonderful love just so that we can grow our faith. Likewise, if we truly believe and have faith in what God has done for us, we will continue to minister. The point is this: God's love for His children never stops, but He loves us because we're His children, not because we did something nice for someone else. So, I offer up this challenge to anyone reading this. Stop reading. Put this book down right now, and tell God thank you. Ask Him to remind you of that moment when you first experienced His precious salvation. Think back to the first time when you heard His voice or the first time that you felt Him wrap His arms around you and whisper "It's ok, I've got you." Go back and find that place where you truly knew that He loved you in a way that you didn't understand, but you knew you didn't have to. And if you've never experienced that, ask Him to let you. Ask Him to make Himself real to you right now. Ask Him to come into your life and make you brand new. It's so simple...why would God, who created everything, hear us ask Him for something like this? The answer is even more simple than the question...because He loves us...and there is no way to comprehend it beyond that.

~

Part 5

A New Covenant

~

As He surveyed the crowd of onlookers that had come to witness the horrible events of that day, His mind flashed back to Eden. The lavish vegetation, the crisp cool waters...His Beloved. He remembered His time strolling through the garden with her and the joy that they both shared. He recalled the majesty of His own glory that reflected in her every smile. It was then that all was perfect. No shame, no pain, no death, but sadly, this was no longer the reality that existed. As this painful thought tore through His mind, the intense pain of the spikes in his wrists and feet forced His mind back to the present. As He hung, beaten and broken on the cross, the horrible and excruciating mechanism of death that was a construct of His own Beloved's mind, He looked down at her. She was there, weeping. The pain of her sorrow was worse than any physical pain He had experienced that day, but He knew this was the only way to fulfill the plan that He had so perfectly placed in motion so many years ago. He knew that it was time for Him to bring an end to the suffering. As He looked at her with earthly eyes one final time, He took every ounce of shame and guilt His Beloved had ever felt, and He placed it on Himself. No sacrifice like this had ever been made in the history of creation, and it was more dreadful than any earthly words could describe. With one final gasp of air, He did exactly what He knew He would have to do eons before ever creating His Beloved, He took every one of her sins to the grave with Him...and He did it gladly.

~

Chapter 17
Prepare The Way

~

Have you ever believed in something so much that it made you look like you weren't really firing on all cylinders? Have you had the opportunity to look at something or someone and see a potential that few others could really see? I'm not talking about a witty idea that may or may not pay off, I'm talking about truly seeing a glimpse of a hell wrecking power and knowing that at some point, a level of victory for God's Kingdom will come forth and manifest itself in a way you've never seen. Few of us are ever lucky enough to really see that, and even fewer are lucky enough to watch it happen. When we recognize this potential, we can't help but do anything we can to make sure that the way is prepared. We whisper to others about it. We see our attitudes shift and our focus grows more intent. We won't let anything disrupt it. Others might begin to question you, but you know deep down in places that only God gets to talk that you're right. After a while, you begin to question yourself. Am I crazy? Am I really doing the right thing here? Am I making too much of this? The enemy knows that what you're doing spells disaster for him and he begins to attack from every angle. The questions that stem from faithfully shepherding God's promised gifts are vast and difficult to answer, but we press on because we know that this is going to be kingdom shaking. We know that if we don't complete our work, then souls may be lost forever.

While some of us may be lucky enough to experience this in our lifetimes, none of us will ever experience this in the same way John the Baptist did. John was born for a specific reason and that reason was to prepare as many people as possible for Jesus Christ. This mission was spoken of John almost 400 years earlier by Isaiah when he said:

A voice of one calling: "In the wilderness prepare the way for the Lord; make straight in the desert a highway for our God.[95]

God planned the timing of John's birth to perfectly coincide with the birth of Christ so that John could proclaim Christ's coming to everyone he could. John's parents were old, his mother barren, but those types of things hadn't stopped God's plan in the past and they weren't going to stop it now. He set His plan in motion all the way back in Eden and this was yet another part of it that He had already worked out. Even before his birth, John was preparing people for Jesus. When Jesus' mother, Mary, visited John's mother, Elizabeth, to tell her the news of her pregnancy, the Bible says that John "leapt" in the womb and that his mother was immediately filled with the Holy Spirit[96]. God ordained John to prepare the way for the Messiah, and John took this charge seriously.

Many people thought John was crazy. He lived in the desert, ate locusts and honey, and wore clothing made of camel hair. He had taken the Nazerite vows, so he never shaved or cut his hair. I'm sure that people who saw this man immediately dismissed him as a loon. But have you ever really looked at this part of John's life to really get an idea of what he was doing? While we can't really relate to the idea of eating locusts and honey or wearing camel hair clothing, the concept of sacrifice shouldn't be foreign to us. John didn't live in the desert because he wanted to look like a crazy doomsdayer, he was out there so that he could focus on Christ. At this time in the world, many prophets spent years in the desert so that they would be isolated from the world and thus able to focus on God. John was no different. He knew that God had called him, and he would not allow the world to stop him. He led a simple life and sought God for everything.

As John's popularity grew, more and more people asked him who he was. They asked if he was Elijah or even the Messiah, but John remained focused. He answered these inquiries humbly, telling the people that "...after me comes one who is more powerful than I, whose sandals I am not worthy to carry."[97] He spoke of baptizing people with water for repentance, but the one following him would "baptize with fire and the Holy Spirit."[98] He never worried about his own standing, only that of Christ. He was perfectly willing to take a backseat. Even when Jesus came and asked John to baptize Him, John replied "I need to be baptized by you..."[99]. Later on, when John's disciples see many of John's followers leave to follow Jesus, they argued. John responded in John 3:29-30:

The bride belongs to the bridegroom. The friend who attends the bridegroom waits and listens for him, and is full of joy when he hears the bridegroom's voice. That joy is mine, and it is now complete. He must become greater; I must become less."

John knew more than anything else in this world that his purpose was to prepare people to hear Christ. John modeled a faith that was displayed in his determination and humility. So, what does this mean for us? Quite simply, it means while we may not all be called to be prophets and preachers, we are all still called. Each and every one of us has experienced the gift of a love so great that we must share it because Christ died for us all. Even if you are reading this and have no relationship with the Creator, He still died for you because He loved you. So how do we spread this wonderful love? We do it by living a life that reflects that love towards others. But wait? If God's love is so unimaginable that we can't even describe it, then how could we, wretched and sinful beings, reflect that love to others. The mirror is a wonderfully simple illustration of this. When you look in a mirror, you see your reflection. There is nothing the mirror has to do for you to see your reflection, it just reflects exactly what is standing before it. Even a broken mirror will reflect the exact parts that pass before it's whole pieces. So, what then does that tell us? We don't have to try to reflect God's glory, we just have to be the mirror. All we have to do is allow Him to be a part of our lives and we can't help but reflect His majesty towards others. Even when we are broken and ashamed, we are pieces that reflect God's light. God's love for His children knows no limitations or constraints, it's just as wonderful and perfect as He is. If God loved us so much that He was willing to lay down His life for us, then it only stands to reason that we are to make sure that every person that we come in contact with knows that they are just as important to Him.

We also have the obligation to nurture the things that God will use while we're here on earth. One of my favorite chapters in the Bible is Exodus 33. I've often referred to this chapter as the "worship leaders chapter". I've clung to this chapter since the early days of my walk with Christ and I've shared it with so many others. While I refer to it as the worship leaders chapter, that doesn't mean that you have to be singing or playing an instrument for it to be applicable to you. In Exodus 33, when the Israelites would make camp, Moses would take the Tent of Meeting and set it up outside the camp. The Bible says that when Moses entered the Tent of Meeting that everyone in the camp would stand at the entrance of their own tent and watch him, and when he went in to talk to God, they began to worship[100]. This is the essence of leading worship...you can't lead it if you're not doing it yourself. While this is indeed relevant and could easily be tied into what we're discussing, it's not the passage that I want you to focus on. You see, Moses was leading the Children of Israel through the wilderness towards the promised land, and he was seeking God's wisdom and guidance, but He still had to go and take care of the day-to-day duties that were required of a man in his position. Moses had to lead God's people, and while he certainly couldn't neglect his own spiritual well-being and relationship with God, God gave him stuff to do also. Enter Joshua. Exodus 33:11 is my favorite scripture and one that I have tried my hardest to model my life around.

The Lord would speak to Moses face to face, as one speaks to a friend. Then Moses would return to the camp, but his young aide Joshua son of Nun did not leave the tent.

When we read this verse, we get excited about how God talked to Moses "as one speaks to a friend". WOW! What an amazing thought! We can enter into God's presence and He will talk with us like we're friends. Yes, very true and wonderful, but read the second part of the verse.

...Joshua son of Nun did not leave the tent.

Let me be clear about something here. I'm not implying that Joshua staying in the tent while Moses went and tended to his duties was more important, but it was equally as important. Moses could never have been a successful leader without Joshua remaining in the presence of God to make sure that someone was crying out on behalf of Moses. Moses had to lead and do the work that God had called him to do, and it was difficult work. Joshua was called to support Moses, and the biggest way he did this was by praying for Moses.

While we are all called to minister the love of our wonderful God to everyone we encounter, many of us are called to other things also. Some are called to preach, to pastor , to sing, to teach, to build, to provide for, and so many other things. Each member of the body has its own specific function, but some of us are also called to support, and to protect, and to guard. Joshua was not only Moses' helper who prayed for him, he was also the captain of Moses' army. He was there to fight the battles and make sure that Moses was around to lead God's people where they needed to go. Joshua had a unique calling, much like John the Baptist did. While John didn't fight with swords in an army, John did fight with his words. When the Pharisees came to watch John baptize people, he went right after them and called them a "brood of vipers" [101] because he knew that they were there to try and disrupt what Christ was ultimately coming to do. John was willing to face jail and death so that Christ's ministry would have as few bumps in the road as possible.

John and Joshua were very different men, in very different times, leading very different roles, in very different situations, but they had one thing in common. They knew more than anything that God had set a job before them and they did everything they could do to make sure that it was completed. Had either of these men thrown up their hands and walked away, God's plan could have rolled right along because God is God and He doesn't get sidetracked, but they were not going to take that chance. They knew that there was someone in their lives that had a calling, and they knew that their own calling was to make sure that that person was able to fulfill theirs. Yes, both of these men did wonderful things in their own right, but it was their willingness to lay down and sacrifice for the calling of someone else that makes them examples. It's in these selfless acts that we are able to see the perfect love of God shining forth.

~
Chapter 18
Almost Perfect Love
~

Perfect love, what a concept that is. I love the word "concept" when we talk about the love of God, because that is essentially what it is. The definition of the word concept is "a general notion or idea", and that is pretty much what God's love is to us. Now don't get upset and start fussing that I'm "generalizing" God's love for us, I'm not. I'm simply pointing out that because of how vast and unimaginable God's love for us truly is, the best that we can do is have a general idea. The most wonderful experiences that we can have with our heavenly father provide us with even more conceptual thoughts about His love as a whole. Why? Because we haven't even scratched the surface of His boundless love. I can't even begin to imagine a love for someone that is greater than the love I have for my kids and my wife, or my closest friends...or cheeseburgers. Someone high five me...you know you're not going to finish this chapter now because you want a cheeseburger.

As much as I do love a good cheeseburger, I'm obviously making a joke in an effort to illustrate the incomprehensible love of our God. What amazes me though is how He places small little examples in our lives that tend to give us just a tiny bit more of an idea of how much He loves us. We still can't grasp it all, mind you, but it's closer. As I was preparing these past few chapters, I was drawn back into some devotions that I had written years ago. Very few people have ever read these, and they were more so writings for me to try and express to God, and to myself, what was on my heart. As I read through these, one of them seemed to genuinely capture the essence of what we are discussing...the unimaginable love that God has for us. So, in full disclosure, I cheated on this chapter and used something I wrote a few years ago after my family and I had just put our Christmas tree up. A few of you have read this original before, but I hope that it still ministers to you because it's in this amazing example that God chose to place the most profound and authoritative example of His love that He could place in a created and flawed human being. That example is a mother's love.

So, what does it mean to be a mom? Over the years I've watched and realized that giving birth was the easy part. When I look and see all the things my wife does to take care of my boys, I'm amazed. I have no idea how she does it. She plays every game, listens to every word of every story, comes up with activities for them to do so they don't get bored, homeschools both of them, and still keeps our home running relatively smooth. On top of all of that, she consistently finds time to study the word of God and stay in prayer for her family. I do help out, but let's face it, I'm an amateur. A while back, out of nowhere, all of these things led me to a question that I can't answer. Can men ever see what Christ did for us the way women do?

The story of Christ's birth has been made so commercial over the years, and we overlook so many aspects of it that it's almost sacrilegious. Every year it gets harder to find any "Christ" in "Christ"mas, but every year I try harder to make sure I remember what we're supposed to be celebrating. Now please, don't get hung up on the "pagan side of Christmas" while you're reading this. I know Christ wasn't born on December 25th and that that date is conveniently close to the winter solstice. I get that, but that's not the point I want to make. We should celebrate the birth of our savior the whole year though, and I do try and do that, but to me, there is nothing wrong with setting aside one day in the year to really focus on it, and that day happens to be December 25th. The fact is, Christ was born, and without his birth, we would have so many bigger issues than whether or not to set the wise men in our nativity seen on the opposite side of the room, so they won't get to Christ for two years.

The point that I really want to make here is actually not about Christ being born, but about the woman who gave birth to him. We all know the story of the Virgin Birth of Christ. Mary was chosen by the Lord to give birth to our Messiah, our Savior, and she accepted that responsibility, and we tend to overlook what she really took on. When you look at your nativity scene do you see the birth of our saving grace and the source of our salvation? Yes, that is exactly what you should see, but take a second look. We see the birth of our Savior, but what we hardly ever see is that it was also the birth of Mary's son. Her flesh and blood - special, in so many ways, but to her, it was her baby boy. What's even more impressive is that she knew the deal. She knew that this little child that she held in her arms had a serious role to play in the lives of people everywhere.

In Luke chapter 2, the story of the birth of Christ, there is a passage that I had never paid much attention to. The shepherd's had begun to tell people about Christ's birth and the talk of the Messiah being born had started to spread. Verse 19, says:

> "But Mary kept all these things and pondered them in her heart."

What do you think was going through her mind? This was her child, her newborn, and he was already being called a king and savior. She had read the scriptures. She knew what Isaiah had written:

> "But He was wounded for our transgressions, He was bruised for our iniquities; The chastisement for our peace was upon Him, And by His stripes we are healed.[102]

Mary knew what her dear son would go though, and she still agreed to take on the task of being Christ's mother.

Later on, in the same chapter of Luke, Mary and Joseph take Jesus to the temple to offer a sacrifice to God and commit Him to the Lord. There was a man named Simeon there who told Mary something that would make any mother cringe. He said:

> "Behold, this Child is destined for the fall and rising of many in Israel, and for a sign which will be spoken against (yes, a sword will pierce through your own soul also), that the thoughts of many hearts may be revealed." [103]

I can't even begin to imagine what Mary felt when she heard those words. Since before she miraculously conceived, she had been told that her Son was going to be killed. How does a mother handle that? How does a Mother go on raising a Son, growing to love him more and more every day, knowing that eventually she is going to have to watch him suffer?

Every day since my children were born, I have worried about them. I have spent countless hours in prayer for them, anointed them with oil so many times I wonder if they are going to have some type of skin condition in that one little spot, and tried to come up with any possible way to allow them to keep their innocence as long as they possibly can. I do all of this because I love them more than anything, but also because it's my job as their father. One thing that I will never be able to do though is love them like their mother does. The love I have for them is greater than anything I can fathom, and yet, it pales in comparison to how my wife looks at them. I can't imagine how my wife would feel if she had to watch one of her baby boys be whipped and beaten and nailed to a cross. The thought of watching her own sons suffer through an agonizing death to save the very people that were doing these things to him is not something I can comprehend. What's even more impressive is that she was willing to be his mother knowing what was going to happen.

A lot can be learned from what Mary did. She watched as her Son sacrificed his life. If you came to me and asked me to lay down my life to save one, or my kid's life to save all...I'm sorry, but only one is going to be saved. The thought of allowing one of them to go through that suffering is more than I could have handled, but Mary did it. I asked my wife once if Christ's death was different to her now that she was a mother and if she could relate to how Mary might have felt. She swallowed one time and simply said "yes". That's all I really needed to hear. I didn't press for details because I knew what she was thinking. Our Savior had a mom, and she had to watch him die.

Over the past years I have found that the birth of Christ was made even more amazing by the willingness of one woman to accept that her son would suffer for all of us. As we have marched through God's master plan to rescue His beloved from the hell that has been unleashed on this world, we have seen many sacrifices, but what Mary did was a little different than the others. Think back to previous chapters and the common theme around how great God's love for us is. He loves us so much that He did everything knowing that we would walk away. Mary's faith was so great because she knew what was going to happen to her baby. That is one of the truest examples of selflessness and obedience I have ever heard of and an example to strive for. In order to be Christ-like, we have to be willing to lay everything down, no matter how hard that might be. He laid down his life, and his mother allowed it. He paid an eternal price for all of us, and all the while she watched and remained faithful to the plan. Mary was a perfect example of God's love reflecting to the world.

~

Chapter 19
Love On Display

~

If I were to ask you to quote a bible verse to me off the top of your head, what would it be? God's holy word is filled with so many different examples of love, encouragement, devotion, protection, and a myriad of other aspects through which our father chooses to redeem himself. It is, after all, His words to us. I'm sure that many of you have your own special verses that you cling to. I've shared several of my favorites with you already and there are so many more that at different times in my life I have clinged to. Psalms 127:1 has reminded me on so many occasions that nothing I can do will effect change if I am not totally sold out to God.

Unless the Lord builds the house, the builders labor in vain. Unless the Lord watches over the city, the guards stand watch in vain.[104]

We've already discussed 2nd Samuel 6:21-22 and how we are supposed to lay down our own pride and simply worship the wonderful God that saw fit to breathe his perfect life into us.

David said to Michal, "It was before the Lord, who chose me rather than your father or anyone from his house when he appointed me ruler over the Lord's people Israel – I will celebrate before the Lord. I will become even more undignified than this, and I will be humiliated in my own eyes. But by these slave girls you spoke of, I will be held in honor." [105]

Isaiah 6 is the immaculate revelation that mortal man has no businesses in the presence of the King of Kings because we are but wretched and sinful beings. Yet in His holiness, there is immaculate grace, and we should be excited to go and tell everyone about it.

In the year that King Uzziah died, I saw the Lord, high and exalted, seated on a throne; and the train of his robe filled the temple. Above him were seraphim, each with six wings: With two wings they covered their faces, with two they covered their feet, and with two they were flying. And they were calling to one another:

"Holy, holy, holy is the Lord Almighty; the whole earth is full of his glory."

At the sound of their voices the doorposts and thresholds shook and the temple was filled with smoke. "Woe to me!" I cried. "I am ruined! For I am a man of unclean lips, and I live among a people of unclean lips, and my eyes have seen the King, the Lord Almighty." Then one of the seraphim flew to me with a live coal in his hand, which he had taken with tongs from the altar. With it he touched my mouth and said, "See, this has touched your lips; your guilt is taken away and your sin atoned for." Then I heard the voice of the Lord saying, "Whom shall I send? And who will go for us?"

And I said, "Here am I. Send me!" [106]

Revelation 4...oh Revelation 4. Can you imagine

it??!!??!! Put this book down right now and read Revelation 4. This chapter is the image that John saw of the throne room of God. Everything bowing down in reverence to our God in all of his brilliant holiness. The words of John in this chapter are but mortal words and in no way can describe the actual glory of what is taking place, but even in his writing, we see that one day, there will be a time that we will bow before our king and worship in ways we can never even comprehend. God's word is amazing, and these are just a few of my favorite passages, but there are so many more. While I'm sure you have your own favorites, there is one that is more well-known than any other verse written in the Bible's entirety. I dare say that if you asked 100 random people to quote a single bible verse to you there would be one that was quoted more than any other. You know which verse I'm talking about don't you? John 3:16:

For God so loved the world that he gave his one and only Son, that whoever believes in him shall not perish but have eternal life.

It's an amazing scripture that really sums up God's promise to us and shows the love that He has for us, even though we've walked away from Him time and time again. So amazing is this one scripture that it can even be viewed as a great fault of we created beings simply because we do not realize what this scripture is representing. A.W. Tozer wrote:

The Christian witness through the centuries has been that

"God so loved the world…"; it remains for us to see that love in the light of God's infinitude. His love is measureless. It is more: it is boundless. It has no bounds because it is not a thing, but a facet of the essential nature of God. His love is something He is, and because He is infinite, that love can enfold the whole created world in itself and have room for ten thousand times ten thousand worlds beside.[107]

What Tozer is saying is that this passage of scripture is far more than a tenant of faith. It is a statement of fact that our God loves us in a way that is so much bigger than anything that we could ever fathom.

The context of this wonderful passage demonstrates much the same. Jesus was speaking with Nicodemus, a Pharisee and a member of the Sanhedrin, a man who was supposed to be versed in scripture and able to teach others. Nicodemus has sought out Jesus because of the works that he had witnessed with his own eyes. Nichodemus knew that Jesus was something special but could not understand what exactly He was.

As they spoke, Jesus laid out for Nicodemus what was taking place right in front of him. The son of God had stepped away from His throne to make sure that each and every one of us had an opportunity to know Him. Now this can easily be spouted as common rhetoric by most American churchgoers, but I challenge you to really consider this. Think back to the beginning of our journey and how God determined to make mankind in His own image. He wanted a relationship with each of us and He created us that way knowing that we would walk away. He then spent years watching His cherished creation grow more and more evil, while all the while, working out a plan that would allow us to come back to Him. And you know what is even more amazing? He already knew that so many of the ones that He would ultimately suffer on the cross for would never return to Him, but He still did it for all of us. It was this truth that Jesus tried to relay to Nicodemus in the third chapter of John, and it's this truth that demonstrates, once again, the amazing love that our God has for us. This is not just a memory verse that we learned as children so that we could "know our bible verses". This is a glimpse into the infinitude of our Holy God and His love.

~

God's infinitude is something that causes us to stumble. It doesn't cause us to stumble because it's fallible, but because we cannot grasp it. We as created beings must measure everything in the way that we can understand. Terms like "eternal", "infinite", and "everlasting" are but constructs of time that we can't really understand, so we just view them as something big. Remember the movie "The Matrix"? I always get a chuckle during the scene when Lawrence Fishburn's character was trying to explain what The Matrix actually was to Keanu Reeves. He says, "If real is what you can feel, smell, taste and see, then 'real' is simply electrical signals interpreted by your brain". I highly doubt that any of the actors or writers of the movie ever thought that this one scene could illustrate our sheer lack of understanding at how big our God is, but it's not that far of a stretch. There is an obvious difference in God's work in our lives than that of a fictional movie about a virtual world. We can feel our God's work in our lives more real than anything, but for man to say that God's love is infinite is simply his way of saying that God is bigger than man himself because we have no way of really knowing how big God is. This limitation of our own minds is what causes us to under sale what God is and what He has done for us.

Christ himself knew that the men around Him could not understand the magnitude and scope of God, so He demonstrated this love in ways that those around Him could potentially grasp. We find one of these examples in John chapter 13. Jesus knows that the time to make the ultimate sacrifice is drawing near, and His time left on earth with His followers is short. As they gather together for one last meal, the Passover meal, Jesus does something that was inexplicable. John 13:4-5 says:

...so he got up from the meal, took off his outer clothing, and wrapped a towel around his waist. After that, he poured water into a basin and began to wash his disciples' feet, drying them with the towel that was wrapped around him.

So, what, He washed their feet, right? The context of this story is not lost on most people who have attended church any time near the Easter season. Washing feet was a job reserved for the servants, but Jesus lowered Himself and washed His disciples feet. Amazing humility, but there is much, much more. John 13:13-15 says:

"You call me 'Teacher' and 'Lord,' and rightly so, for that is what I am. Now that I, your Lord and Teacher, have washed your feet, you also should wash one another's feet. I have set

you an example that you should do as I have done for you."

What Jesus is telling His disciples is that if you really want to know my love, then try to love others the way I love you. We know that isn't possible, and so did Jesus, but the act of washing someone's feet could be done by anyone. It was a job reserved for a servant, which meant there was no special training, no special anointing, no special calling, no special title that was required. The only thing that was required to wash someone's feet was love and humility. This amazing love that Jesus displayed to His disciples was His way of reminding them on one simple thing. He was reminding them that what He was about to do for them, only He could do, but they could make sure that everyone they encountered knew about the love that He had for them. And so can we.

~

Chapter 20
Feed My Sheep

~

Over the past two months, I have struggled to figure out what to say from this point on. Not only is writer's block a real thing, the concept of trying to convey anything that would do the sacrifice of our savior justice is a struggle. I've sat down at my computer multiple mornings and began typing only to get a page or two in and realize that what I was putting on the pages was not quite the direction I needed to go in. I even typed the phrase "examples of God's love" into Google and read about 15 different articles by different people looking for ideas. Each time I would read one and get a little bit of inspiration, I would hit a wall and realize that that wasn't it either. A friend of mine told me once, after forgetting what he was going to say, that that was just wisdom. It's grown into a great joke anytime one of us fumbles a conversation, but there is a bit of truth in that statement. So, I'm going to just chalk all of those false starts up to wisdom. I guess the bright side of this is that I have the beginnings of about ten or twelve individual devotions on the topic of Christ's death and the love He displayed for us that may be of use in the future, who knows.

As much as I would love to talk about the day Christ was crucified in graphic and wonderful detail, I just can't do it. There are plenty of movies, books, and other writings that can do a much better job at describing what our Lord went through that day and pull the desired emotional response out of you. I'm not an author. Everything that you've read in the pages leading up to this, and everything you will read afterward, are little more than glorified journal entries compiled in the hopes that someone would be ministered to by reading them. I have no intention of trying to make you sad as you think about Jesus' death and react to an emotion. We allow our emotions to dictate far too much of our lives already, and while emotion can be a wonderful thing, and there is absolutely nothing wrong with crying when we think about what Jesus did for us, it's not the emotion that draws us close to Him. I can't, in good conscience, sit here and pander to your emotions in the hope that you will shed a tear because the truth is that Christ did die for us, but He did not die for us so that we would feel sorry for Him. He sacrificed everything for us so that we could be free from hell and sin, and while it was horrific from a human perspective, it was no accident. There was no misfortune or bad luck that He didn't expect. Each lash of the whip landed exactly where He knew it would land. What He did was intentional.

I recently had an opportunity to speak to our church youth group about being intentional in our relationship with God. Spending time with God even though we may not feel like it fills our heart with His word and allows us to lean into Him and know that He will never forsake us. I'm not sure if you've ever spoken to a room full of teenagers before but to give you an example of what it's like, find the biggest, emptiest room in your house and go ask a question you expect an answer too.

I was lucky in that I had one who would give me a quick "woo" on occasion, but if you want to talk about being intentional, prepare notes that will span 20 minutes of "conversation" with a room full of teenagers.

I kid, a little because our church has a great group of young people and it's a lot of fun to get to work with them, but teenagers are an awesome example of what the other side of being intentional in a relationship requires. My kids are both younger, and they still look at dad like he can do anything in the world. Honestly, the fact that I can build a website or a mobile app makes my ten year old think that I could help him create the company to dethrone Apple. In a few years though, he's going to realize that dad is a huge mess. As a teenager, he's going to look at me and see the chinks in the armor. He'll see the failures and the faults. He'll be able to recognize the struggles. He'll never quite look at me the same way he does now, and while that's ok that is also where being intentional in my relationship with him will be so important. Things like making sure to tell him I love him a little more often even though He doesn't want to hear it, or doing a few extra small, nice things on occasion for him even though he'll be so opposed to me drawing attention to us are critical. I have to take advantage of any conversation just to be sure he knows that I'm always there to talk to him. There will be times that I may be doing all of these things knowing that they will be met with unappreciation, but that's ok because my love for him is more important than his approval of me. These are things that we as adults take for granted because we understand that we love our kids more than anything. Our kids don't always see things the way we see them though, so we have to be intentional in what we're doing so that when they look back, they're able to say "Wow, dad loved me, even when I didn't make it easy on him." This is the example that Christ laid out for us. Loving our children and those around us the way that Christ loved us will be met with a lot of heartaches. Others may not understand the way we love them, but just like we know that we may be met with a small amount of rejection, Christ knew He would be met with rejection on a whole new level and He still sacrificed everything for us.

While we are obviously imperfect in our efforts to show the ones that we love how much we love them, luckily for us, God isn't. The intentionality that God had in His relationship with us is amazing. When we look at what He did for us on the cross as well as leading up to the cross, it makes us realize even more that He was after one thing, us.

A few weeks ago, I was drinking my coffee and reading through a devotional that I had recently started. That morning's reading was not particularly grabbing my attention and I was, in the back of my mind, thinking about how ready I was to wrap up that chapter and get on with my day. I was really having to be intentional about my reading that morning. I'm sure you can relate to those days when you feel like you're just going through the motions without much heart behind it. We have all had those days when it seems like no matter how good the content, you just can't seem to latch on to what it is you're doing. As I was truly skimming the last few pages, one sentence caught my attention.

"The things God deposits in your spirit in the midst of suffering, are the same things that someday other people will desperately need."[108]

I sat there for a moment and thought about this sentence and then continued on. A paragraph or so later I found myself moving back to this sentence. Again, I moved away only to drift back. This one sentence stuck with me. Why? This year has been a struggle for many of us, myself included, but I will be the first to admit that I have been blessed. While I have had to fight my own spiritual battles, there are so many others out there that have suffered far more than I have in these seasons. Why was this one sentence eating at my insides? I spent the day rolling this around in my mind trying to figure out exactly why this one statement had attached itself to me in the way it had. What was God trying to remind me of? I shared the passage with a few friends and did the obligatory share on social media. I hoped someone would see it and be encouraged or drop some insight on me that I didn't have, but ultimately, I still had no answer about what God was trying to show me. I spent days thinking about this one sentence and then it happened...I forgot about it and moved on. See what I did there? You thought there was some great revelation coming, didn't you? To be honest with you, I'm far more amused by that than any of you probably are.

As funny as that was, at least to me, let me get back to

the point at hand. I'm going to let you in on something that I'm convinced is one of the most frustrating things about being a follower of Christ. His timing is not our timing. Earth-shattering, right? I suspect we've all experienced this morsel of spiritual truth in some way or another. You're certain that God has something for you. Maybe you're even holding onto a promise that He so clearly gave you, but you just can't seem to get across that Jordan River. The simple truth is that when God decides that He wants to share something with you, very rarely are you going to just "get it". Oftentimes, you will get the seed of whatever it is He is trying to grow in you and then it's up to you to cultivate and nourish that seed to see it turn into fruit. How do we nourish that seed? We seek God, constantly. We stay in His word and talk to Him, even when we don't want to. We remain intentional about our relationship with Him knowing that even when we feel like we are not getting anywhere we are filing things away for a later battle. The more we are in the word of God, the more we can lean on His promises to us when things look dark. The more we're focused on hearing what God is saying, even when we think it doesn't apply, the more equipped we are to recognize the next piece of what God is trying to show us.

As I have been working on this last section, I've had Peter on my mind a lot. Peter was a rock star disciple. He followed Jesus so adamantly that he oftentimes got a bit too bold. How many other people actually had the nerve to scold Jesus like Peter did when Jesus predicted His own death[109]? Peter was the first disciple to call Jesus the son of God[110], and he was one of Jesus' closest friends and companions.

What I've been pondering lately was not Peter's enthusiastic devotion to Christ, but the night that he denied Jesus. Not so much in the sense of Peter being weak and afraid, but from Jesus' perspective. When Jesus became fully man, He had to endure temptation. It was not just in the wilderness after fasting that He was tempted but throughout his entire ministry. Jesus had to constantly guard His own heart from the temptation of proving himself right. Jesus could have called down all of Heaven in front of the entire Sanhedrin and they would have understood who He was immediately. They would have known that He was the Messiah, but that wouldn't have required faith on their parts...and they may not have crucified Him. We rarely think about why Jesus handled situations the way He did. Consider what would have happened had Jesus presented himself in all of his heavenly glory to everyone. He wouldn't have been rejected and there would have been no bloodshed. We would have been relegated to an eternity of separation from Him. Jesus had a plan, and that plan was executed to perfection.

So what does Jesus being tempted have to do with Peter's denial? Think about the fully human side of Jesus for a moment. How would you have felt, facing one of the toughest trials of your life, knowing so much more was coming, and then having to experience one of your closest friends betray you? Imagine the look on Jesus' face in Luke 22 when Peter denied Jesus for the third time. Why do I think this upset Jesus so much? Because it was Peter. Jesus may have been troubled by what Judas did, but Judas was not one of Jesus' closest friends, Peter was.

Peter was the guy who trusted Jesus enough to get out of a boat in the middle of a raging storm and believe that he was going to walk on water, and he did! It may have only been for a few steps, but he did it! No one else got out of the boat. And yeah, he sank a few steps later because he took his eyes off of Jesus, but he still had enough trust in Jesus to step over the side of that boat. He had monster faith!

Peter was the same person that Jesus took with Him to the transfiguration and let him witness the most amazing display that anyone on Earth at the time had ever experienced. Peter saw Jesus, fully man, being fully God. Peter actually heard the voice of God the Father audibly speak. He saw Moses and Elijah. He witnessed something that only two other people got to witness!

Peter, the friend that Jesus took to the prayer war in the garden with him. When Jesus knew that it was almost time to face the end and He was "troubled in His spirit", He took Peter and said, "pray"! You don't ask the ones that you don't believe in or trust to pray for you or with you. We may make prayer requests to a group but when we really need soldiering in the spiritual battle that's personal. Jesus believed in Peter that much!

When Peter denied knowing Christ, imagine how Jesus felt. Imagine the heart-wrenching pain he felt knowing that one of his most beloved friends refused to even acknowledge Him. Jesus could have broken free of His restraints easily and called Peter out, but He didn't. He faced His accusers, the ones He came to save, with the added pain of one of His best friends breaking His heart.

Why did it hurt so bad? Because it was Peter! The first time Peter met Jesus; Jesus called him "the rock". Peter was the first disciple that Jesus called to follow Him. Jesus loved Peter, invested in Peter, pushed Peter to be a better person, taught Peter, and prayed for Peter. Jesus ate dinner with Peter, hung out with Peter, and talked with Peter. And while Peter was unsophisticated and even crude at times, he was all heart. He so aggressively loved Jesus that sometimes Jesus had to tell him to ease off the throttle a bit and think about what he was doing or saying. Peter was more than a disciple; Peter was Jesus' friend.

Peter's denial of Jesus and how that made Jesus feel has been swirling around in my head the past few weeks, but that's not necessarily the point I'm going for here. What I want you to see in this is the restoration that Jesus gave to Peter. When Peter heard the rooster crow and Jesus looked at him, Luke 22 says that Peter ran out of the gates and "wept bitterly". Those tears changed Peter forever. The tears that Peter shed made him see that he was not there to save Jesus, but that Jesus was there to save Him.

Peter's restoration process took a few days. He didn't just stop crying and stand up with everything figured out. He still had to watch his friend be crucified and he still had to carry the guilt of what he had done with him. It wasn't until after Jesus' resurrection that we see the commission given to Peter that would rock the world unlike anything short of Jesus Himself. The gospel of John outlines a tinder conversation between Christ and Peter. Jesus asks Peter three different times, "Peter, do you love me more than these?". Each time he is asked, Peter responds in the affirmative, but he responds differently the third time. When Jesus asks Peter the third time, Peter answers, "Lord, you know all things; you know that I love you[111].". This answer finally opened Peter's eyes to the revelation that no matter how imperfect our love is, Christ's love will never fail. Our God loves us perfectly and without a perfect love we would have been rejected. That night at Caiaphas' home Jesus, though hurt, knew Peter loved Him. He knew that Peter, while weak, still loved his friend and would ultimately become "the rock" that Jesus had already told him he would be. He also knew that Peter couldn't love Him the way that He loved Peter. That simply wasn't possible. So Jesus would die for Peter and for us so that we could be forever embraced in that perfect love and never have to wonder if we were loved.

The things God deposits in your spirit in the midst of suffering, are the same things that someday other people will desperately need. Remember that line from earlier? Who better than Peter to bring that to life? Who better than the broken man who had just turned his back on his friend and watched him be ushered to death to illustrate that point? Peter learned something in his tears that night that he would take with him all the way to his death. He learned that no matter what we do our God is full of love for us. A love that we can't understand or explain, but it's real. It's so real that no matter what Peter faced he was going to make sure that everyone heard about that love.

We don't always win our battles. In fact, we're going to lose so many that it's embarrassing if we think back on them. There will be times when we look back on our lives and realize that we denied Christ. Be it in words or deeds, we will deny Christ in our lives. I'm sorry to be the one to point this out, but it will happen more than once. How can we deny Christ if we claim to love Him? The answer is because our love is imperfect. While our imperfect love is no excuse for our sin it is the thing that allows us to cherish the perfect love of our Heavenly Father. The father who loves us in ways we can never begin to imagine. We fail in so many ways, but Jesus keeps coming back and saying "do you love me? Then feed my sheep." He doesn't put us on the sideline when we falter, He puts us right back into the battle. He keeps putting us into situations where warfare is inevitable. He keeps harvesting the fruit that has been planted by those trials and we are able to see new people step into His kingdom every day. He knows we will fail and that's why He died for us. He knew we would deny Him again, but He also knew that we were going to look at him, grieved in our own spirit, and say "You KNOW that I love you!". We have to be able to hold on to the fact that Jesus, for each time we deny Him, is going to come right back to us, with a gentle smile, and say "Do you love me more than these?" And when He does, we have to be able to let Him love us because it's only in His perfect love that we can accomplish what He has placed us on this earth to do...tell everyone we meet that He loves them too.

~

Part 6

The Time Is Near

~

Perched high above the heavens, He sat patiently watching and waiting. He knew that the time was near and He only awaited one final thing. She was always in His sight, His Beloved. He never removed His watchful gaze from her, and she never took her eyes off of Him. She knew Him the way she once had, and it delighted Him in ways that words could not explain. He watched as evil surrounded her, yet she remained faithful to Him. Though she tripped and stumbled, she never turned her back on Him. She never walked away. She clung to His words, she held onto His promises, and she told everyone that would listen about Him. His eyes shone with what could only be described as true love as He watched Her preparing herself, making sure that she was ready for Him to return to her. His spirit had protected and guided her, and He knew that the time was near. Then, in a voice filled with the utmost purity and innocence, a voice of one redeemed, He heard her say "Come, Lord Jesus." He rose from His throne and turned and faced His father. Eternities past had led to this one moment. The final piece of the most perfect rescue plan fell into place as His father smiled at Him and said "Son, go and get your Bride."

~

Chapter 21
It's Not To Late

~

Well, we have arrived at the end of our journey. I offer you a lighthearted congratulations for making it to the end. The peaks and valleys of my mind's ramblings are not for the faint of heart. I must say that this has been an interesting journey for me as well. As I've studied and written, and re written, and re written again, I've uncovered so many things that I have turned inward, ways to examine my own life and my own application of the very points that I am trying to convey to you.

I learned a few years back that just because God is teaching you something that everyone else may not be in the same place you are. Everyone else may not be ready to latch on to what you've been shown. I try to keep this in mind as I write, but this message was a little different. Why? Because this message is for everyone, everywhere, at any time. You see, God will reveal things to you in the time that He knows that you can handle them and not everyone is ready to hear each revelation that you may receive. However, the one thing that we should never question is whether someone is ready to hear about the love of our savior. In fact, I would suggest that we should, with the utmost urgency, be telling everyone we can about that love with the understanding that we are not playing a game. We are dealing with eternity. With that in mind, I would like to pose two questions.

The first question is are you ready to stand before Jesus and give an account of your life? Make no mistake about it, you will have to do this. The Bible says in Philippians

...every knee should bow, in heaven and on earth and under the earth, and every tongue acknowledge that Jesus Christ is Lord, to the glory of God the Father.[112]

We will have to stand before God and give an account of what we've done. Imagine standing before our God's throne, and if you could, look around and to see everyone that you've ever come in contact within your life. How many of them will come to you, glorious expressions on their face and say "Thank you! Your life, your words, your dedication to our king was a light to me. It led me to my own relationship with Him. I would not be here if it was not for you."? What an amazing thought!! But what about the others? How many will come to you and say the exact opposite? How many, with anguish on their faces, will say "Why didn't you tell me?!!! Why didn't you try?! Why didn't you do everything you could to make sure that I knew about Him?!! Why didn't you just let a small piece of Him shine through you so that I would see?"? It's this line of people that brings tears to my eyes even as I write this. How many people have I encountered that I didn't let know about Christ and will I ever get that chance again? I can only pray that another can pick up the ball that I dropped on so many occasions. Whether we have a relationship with Christ or not we will all stand before Him and declare that He is the Lord. And what follows that declaration is the most important thing you will ever hear. Will you hear "Well done, my good and faithful servant"? Or will you hear "Depart from me, for I never knew you"? This is not a joke, it is serious, and the time for a decision is now.

It's that seriousness that leads me to my second question. Do you know Jesus? Do you know Him the way that we've talked about for the last however many pages? Do you have a relationship with Him where you experience His heartwarming love day in and day out? Do you know that He loves you? No matter what you've done or what has been done to you, He loves you more than anything. Romans says:

For I am convinced that neither death nor life, neither angels nor demons, neither the present nor the future, nor any powers, neither height nor depth, nor anything else in all creation, will be able to separate us from the love of God that is in Christ Jesus our Lord.[113]

Do you understand what this scripture is telling you? It's telling you that absolutely nothing can stand in the way of God's love. You were bought with a price that only a perfectly loving God could pay, and that price was paid gladly. Nothing, and I do mean nothing, can keep you from Him. Any thought that you are not worthy of His love is a lie. Any notion that you are too damaged or too far gone is a wretched untruth. Frank Peretti wrote:

No amount of lies, no matter how cleverly couched, will ever outstrip or outlast God's truth, nor will any lie ever outreach

His grace.[114]

His grace is boundless, His mercy is endless, and His love is eternal. I want to be very clear about something, this is not a decision to save you from Hell. Yes, that comes with it, but this is a decision to enter into a relationship that is more rewarding than anything our earthly minds can create or understand. This decision is to come home, back to the arms of the King of Kings, to be one of His children who is loved and adored no matter what has taken place in the past. He is there, right now, just waiting for you to ask Him to be a part of your life. I love the old hymn, Just As I Am:

> *Just as I am, Thou wilt receive*
> *Wilt welcome, pardon, cleanse, relieve*
> *Because Thy promise I believe*
> *O Lamb of God, I come, I come*

"O Lamb of God, I come". It's that simple. He's there waiting for you right now. Waiting to cleanse you of shame, of sin, of guilt. He's waiting to relieve you of your burdens. Will life be perfect after, no, but you will have the most perfect Savior, the most perfect Lord, the most perfect King, and the most perfect Father that you could ever imagine right beside you through everything you face moving forward. All you have to do is ask Him. There is no special prayer, no special quote, no special place. Just ask Him to be a part of your life. Tell Him that you want to experience His love and live for Him. Don't wait. This is the most important decision that you will ever make.

~

Lord, I confess my sins to you and ask for your forgiveness.
I pray you would come to be the Lord of my life today and make me a new creation. I believe that you died and rose again and through your sacrifice I am made clean.

~

~

REFERENCES

~

[1] 1 John 4:19 (New International Version)
[2] Genesis 1:1 (New International Version)
[3] Genesis 1:26 (New International Version)
[4] James Hilton, *The Lost Horizon*
[5] Home, *The Odyssey*
[6] Genesis 3:7 (New International Version)
[7] Genesis 3:14-19 (New International Version)
[8] Genesis 3:23-24 (New International Version)
[9] Genesis 5:24 (New International Version)
[10] 2nd Kings 2:11 (New International Version)
[11] Genesis 6:8 (New International Version)
[12] Genesis 9:11 (New International Version)
[13] Joshua 24:2 (New International Version)
[14] Genesis 14:18-20 (New International Version)
[15] Hebrews 7:22 (New International Version)
[16] Genesis 15:9 (New International Version)
[17] Genesis 15:11 (New International Version)
[18] Genesis 15:12-21 (New International Version)
[19] Genesis 16 (New International Version)
[20] Genesis 17:3-8 (New International Version)
[21] Genesis 21:1-5 (New International Version)
[22] Genesis 22:2 (New International Version)
[23] Genesis 22:2-5 (New International Version)
[24] Genesis 22:6 (New International Version)
[25] Genesis 22:7 (New International Version)
[26] Genesis 22:11-13 (New International Version)
[27] Genesis 17:19 (New International Version)
[28] Genesis 25:29-34 (New International Version)
[29] Genesis 24:15 (New International Version)

[63] 1 Samuel 17:17-19 (New International Version)
[64] 1 Samuel 18:2-5 (New International Version)
[65] 1 Samuel 18:7 (New International Version)
[66] 1 Samuel 24:3-4 (New International Version)
[67] 1 Samuel 24:4 (New International Version)
[68] 1 Samuel 16:13 (New International Version)
[69] 1 Samuel 24:6 (New International Version)
[70] 1 Samuel 24:8 (New International Version)
[71] Genesis 29:15-30 (New International Version)
[72] Genesis 29:31 (New International Version)
[73] Genesis 29:32 (New International Version)
[74] Genesis 29:33 (New International Version)
[75] Genesis 29:34 (New International Version)
[76] Genesis 29:35 (New International Version)
[77] Genesis 37:26-27 (New International Version)
[78] Genesis 38:12-30 (New International Version)
[79] Genesis 43:8-9 (New International Version)
[80] Genesis 43:34 (New International Version)
[81] Genesis 44:33 (New International Version)
[82] Genesis 49:8-12 (New International Version)
[83] 2 Samuel 5:6-25 (New International Version)
[84] 2 Samuel 6:6-7 (New International Version)
[85] 2 Samuel 6:9 (New International Version)
[86] 2 Samuel 6:13 (New International Version)
[87] 2 Samuel 6:14 (New International Version)
[88] 2 Samuel 6:20 (New International Version)
[89] William J. Dumbrell, Covenant and Creation: A Theology of Old Testament Covenants
[90] 2nd Samuel 7:2 (New International Version)
[91] Romans 7:15 (New International Version)
[92] Matthew 1:17 (New International Version)
[93] Matthew 2:16 (New International Version)
[94] James 2:18-26 (New International Version)

[95]Isaiah 40:3 (New International Version)
[96]Luke 1:41 (New International Version)
[97]Matthew 3:11 (New International Version)
[98]Matthew 3:11(New International Version)
[99]Matthew 3:14 (New International Version)
[100]Exodus 33:8-11 (New International Version)
[101]Matthew 3:7 (New International Version)
[102]Isaiah 53:5 (New International Version)
[103]Luke 2:34-35 (New International Version)
[104]Psalm 127:1 (New International Version)
[105]2nd Samual 6:21-22 (New International Version)
[106]Isaiah 6:1-8 (New International Version)
[107]A.W. Tozer, *Knowledge of the Holy*
[108]Levi Lusko, *Taking Back Your Life*
[109]Mark 8:32 (New International Version)
[110]Mark 8:29 (New International Version)
[111]John 21:17 (New International Version)
[112]Philippians 2:10-11(New International Version)
[113]Romans 8:38-39 (New International Version)
[114]Frank Peretti, *Piercing the Darkness*

Made in the USA
Coppell, TX
15 September 2023

21606640R00095